Go ride first.

Stovepiper Books Media

mikedaily.bandcamp.com

ISBN: 978-0-9642339-3-5

Copyright © 2020 by Mike Daily

Cover Design, Illustrations, and Book Layout
by Nathan Powell
nmp@nathanpowelldesign.com

Proofreading by Ryan Schierling,
Monkey Meets The Blowtorch

Second Printing Forever

This is a work of fiction.

Printed in the U.S.A.

For
Cameron Pierce

what's the point of a city you cant crush

P.O.S
"They Can't Come (feat. Sims),"
We Don't Even Live Here (2012)

Foreword

Moon Babes of Bicycle City—Inspirations and references and dialogue that only a rider like Mike Daily could create, representing BMX Freestyle in the uniquely creative way, of which these unrecreatable days of the spawning of BMX Freestyle do DESERVE...!

Moon Babes highlights some of the purest moments of BMX Freestyle history in an equally creative way as were the groundbreakingly creative events and parts and tricks about which it was written! Including, but not limited to the valuable inclusions of Steve Bennett, Rocket from the Crypt, 43, Swirling Zagnuts, the so-stylish "Crews", and sadly, Pearl Jam (haha)...

Yet with all the deep BMX knowledge and references aside, I'm still left with the burning question: do Tuff Wheels straighten in the FREEZER?

Ron W
Santa Cruz, California
January 28, 2020

Ron W
Beijing 2008
Photo by Lew

Readers ready?
Turn the page.

Chapter One

New Mexico, 2019

South of Roswell, north of Hope, east of an Apache reservation, west of Dexter and Lake Arthur lies Bicycle City, New Mexico.
   Oh.
   Morning.
   Mid-October.
   Bangin' Elbows Road.
   Rodderick Moon and Mick O'Grady are "flat-out haulin' bazoonies" in Rodd's bikecar replica of a '76 Chrysler Cordoba.
   Two sets of Cook cranks instead of a motor.
   Skyway Tuff Wheels with stadium tires courtesy of Tioga.
   Rodd says the body is made of recycled aluminum cans of Jolt Cola.
   He sips day-glo soda.
   Rodd returns the Rad Cup-coozy'd bottle to the ACS Rotor beverage holder.
   Taped to the dashboard is a flyer for Miami Hopper yoga.

Rodd's wardrobe is composed of collectible clothing: Life's a Beach skull and crossbones cap and sneakers, Bad Otis Link sleeveless, thrift store shorts, Vision hip pack and socks, Swatches.

He says he has a watch to keep track of each of his daughters: Suzue, Araya, and Ukai Moon.

They're in three different time zones.

Their mom's home.

She'll be headin' off to work soon.

"What's her name?" Mick asks.

"Chatauqua. Chatauqua Moon. Everyone calls her Chat. Except a total poser on a Milwaukee Bruiser 'trick track' who calls her The Cougar on the Jag."

"Your wife has a Jag?"

Rodd nods.

"Team Jag. Keep pedalin' like Lee Medlin. This ain't a sidehack!"

"Thank you Gary Littlejohn," Mick says.

He's yawning for oxygen.

Rodd laughs.

Odor of manure in the air from the creameries.

Piñon smoke from a chimney.

Reminds Mick of PA.

And Lock Haven University.

He's wearing a P.O.S shirt, jeans, vegan belt with a Def Jux buckle, Nike DOOM Dunks with Aesop Rock laces.

Sun is blazing.

They're out of coconut water and Gatorade.

Can he slake his thirst at the next emergency eye wash station?

The Schwinn Scrambler breakfast plates and Muscle Power shakes they had at Starting Gate Café burned off long ago.

Mick doesn't recall signing up for all this cardio.

His eyes were bigger than his thighs, he guesses.

Session, he sees.

Jam circle outside an arcade.

Guy on a chrome Ozone megaspins to a McApplecrate and waves.

"Bananas," Mick says.

He breaks one off, hands it to Rodd.

"Thank you, O'Grady."

"You're welcome. So what does it take to become a 'Moon Babe' of Bicycle City? Wait. Don't tell me. Big hair?"

"*Massive* air," Rodd says.

"'Hair', I said."

"Moon Babes is a bike club like any other. You have to be asked to join. Chosen."

"I thought that was gangs," Mick says. "And the mob."

They pass the jam circle.

Rodd looks at him.

"Bike club."

Chapter Two

Shut-ins.

Rodd and Mick pedal in unison past pueblos in ruins.

Rodd is talking.

"Garrido's got a connection in Auburn Hills, Michigan, he says. What could be better than Corinthian leather to cover these front bucket seats? 'Rad Pads,' I said to him. 'Rad Pads, my friend.' Patterson, Pro Neck, Robinson, DG, Diamond Back. I had all my vinyl packed in gym bags at the shop. I unzipped one and he reached in at random, pulled out a Torker pad. Frank Garrido was sponsored by Torker! Him and Dale Perez. That sidehack they rode at Pipeline Skatepark? It was a Webco with Bottema forks. Shinglehead sent me photos of a JMC Racing commemorative quilt someone had made and I thought it would be great if we did the same thing for these seats. Garrido goes, 'That's gonna be hot. You're gonna need air conditioning.' I didn't know about A/C at the time but I did know I was gonna need a seamstress. And I knew just the girl to go to: Genevieve Fennelseed. If I could find her."

"Whoa," Mick says.

"I know—amusing name, eh? 'Genevieve Fennelseed'? Her friends call her 'Jean'. Crazy kids these days."

"No," Mick says. "Whoa!"

"'Whoa' what?"
"There's a skinhead bodybuilder about to bunnyhop a Bully with a bashguard—"
"What?"
"—onto us!"
Impact to the roof of the hardtop coupe.
Mick feels the door panel is padded, too.
They're tipped sideways on two wheels.
Slow motion sensation for a second.
Rodd lands it.
"*Adam-12!*" he yells. "Wasn't that where the cars went up on two wheels? No! *Dukes of Hazzard*! *Knight Rider*!"
He's looking into the rear-view mirror.
He picks up a reporter-style microphone.
It has MTV stickers on it.
"*Kerrang*!" he bellows over a loudspeaker. "Bloody hellion! Ease-up, mate! Mate?"
He keeps looking.
"He's not gettin' up, gang! Let's hear it for him! Come on, Bicycle City! Make some noise!"
Rodd returns the microphone to the center console.
The dashboard above his chopped Peregrine Q handlebars and ODI Mushroom II grips is slick from spilled soda.
"Good thing my pop was a wounded soldier," he says. "My banana fell though. I lost it. Now would be a good time to throw stickers, O'Grady. Open the glove box."
There aren't many onlookers on the scene that Mick can see.
The ones that are, are riding.
"Throw stickers? To who?"
"To whom it may concern."
The glove box door has a gold Cordoba logo on it.
Mick opens the door.
The compartment is packed with stickers in stacks: Jive Handles "Live, Thrive, Jive," Anarchic Adjustment, GT.

"Neon 'Crack 'n Peel' Club Homeboy? Wow. Where did you get these?"

"They're re-pops. Reproductions. Not those." Rodd grabs a different stack. He hands it to Mick. "These."

Mick reads:

"You made stickers."

"Ron Wilkerson made stickers. Toss 'em."

"All of 'em?"

"Yeah, I got a ton of 'em. And the contest is tomorrow."

Mick presses the down arrow and lowers the Plexiglas window.

He rolls the rubber band off the stack.

He tosses the stickers.

They scatter.

Flutter.

He raises the window.

Rodd turns up the A/C.

Mick looks into the side-view mirror.

Riders are going for them, he notices.

A roadie, even, has stopped and stooped.

Bearded roadie.

"Get a good gander, O'Grady. Because tomorrow mornin' these side mirrors are gettin' knocked off by a General rider from New York—General Kearney. He'll be usin' a two-by-four for authenticity. Ceremony. Then it's gettin' duct-taped and spray-painted. That's why the colorway is primer grey at the moment. Hand me those wet weather gloves, please."

"JT wet weather gloves in a glove compartment! This is startin' to make some sense."

"Don't Die Wondering," Rodd says, referencing the Vision Street Wear sticker on the ash tray.

Mick laughs.

"Actually, I'll just use this—"

Rodd un-does the quick release on his Vision hip sack and uses it to wipe the windshield and dash.

"Vision Street Wear," Mick says. "The quicker picker-upper."

"Speakin' of 'quicker picker-uppers,' there's a place up here that has chicks who do cherrypickers."

Mick isn't interested, he says. Not unless they do angel dust.

"It's called Thrusters," Rodd says. "Elina's Thrusters."

No thanks. Tempting, but he'll decline.

Rodd wants to know how Mick can not be interested! Cherrypickers! Barspin cherrypickers!

Mick says he doesn't have cash for it, anyway.

What if Mick is sponsored? Factory sponsored?

Mick asks Rodd what he meant by that.

Rodd meant that he owns the establishment.

Mick is not a fan of organized crime.

Rodd laughs and says that's what Mick says, but Rodd thinks he might be.

Rodd thinks Mick might be a fan of organized crime?

Rodd thinks Mick might be interested.

Are they Moon Babes?

They're not Moon Babes, no. Is Mick crazy? Thrusters, brother. The instant replays are radibonzical.

Stop, Mick says.

No, Rodd says. It's too early. They're headin' straight to the shop. Mick's pickin' out a build then they're shreddin'. Has he seen the Fall catalog?

Yes, Mick wants the Panda. The R.C. Alderman Replica Panda Pro-Am.

Fantastic choice, Rodd says.

They pedal past Thrusters.

Elina's Thrusters.

Chapter Three

Rodd says he called it what it was: Retire. Retire Bikes. Moon Babes Retire Bikes. That was the impetus. Genesis, whatever. When they started the shop, it was a tire dealership. The O's in "Moon" on the sign are solid rubber hoops from penny-farthings. Made in Argentina.

"So when did you and Chat move to New Mexico?" Mick asks.

"Right after that first Meet the Street contest I met you at in Santee," Rodd says. "April 30, 1988. We had Suzue with us. Chat was pregnant with Araya."

"Is that how you pronounce it? 'Ah-*rye*-yuh'? I always thought it was 'Ah-*ray*-uh' rims. I'm from York, PA, what can I say?"

"A lot of hicks say it like that."

"I'll tell Dizz Hicks you said that."

"Now you know the correct pronunciation."

"Araya," Mick says. "Lovely. I heard Dizz is gonna be here tomorrow."

"Yeah. Him and Ceppie Maes."

"Who made those paper dolls of them?"

"Araya did," Rodd says. "She'll be back from Cali tomorrow. She works at Ride-Thru Hookah Express, if you're interested."

"I'm sober. Eight years."

"I know. You told me."

"Responsible energy now," Mick says.

Rodd parks the bikecar in front of Moon Babes Retire Bikes.

"Get out."

Chapter Four

Moon Babes headquarters.
Mick guzzles a rain forest spring water.
He drops the plastic bottle into a recycling bin covered with vintage stickers.
The Moon family's youngest daughter, Ukai—15, Rodd had said outside—is sitting behind the shop's glass case counter.
She's reading a magazine.
Mick sees it's a BMX mag. *Undergrounders*. He says he hasn't seen that one yet. Must be the latest issue.
"It is," Rodd says. "We just got 'em in."
Ukai is wearing a tilted-back black mesh cap. It says "MOON BABES" in yellow on the front and "BICYCLE CITY" in red on green under the bill. M&M Apparel Kuwahara jersey with padded elbows.
"Kuwahara is Japanese for 'mulberry meadows'," Mick says to Ukai.
"She knows," Rodd says.
"You knew that?" Mick asks Ukai.
She nods.
"Ukai's best friend—her 'BFF'—is Heather Mulberry Meadows," Rodd says. "Remember Heath Meadows?"
"No."

"He raced for Kuwahara. Co-factory Kuwahara. They moved here from Davis when we did. We migrated from the most bicycle-friendly city to the most car-unfriendly one in the world: BC! You saw what that dude tried to do to my bikecar. We're more concerned with keepin' cars out than we are with public safety. I like that about us though. We're enclosed like a self-addressed stamped envelope. Remember those? Self-addressed stamped envelopes?"

"Yes, I do."

"That's how I used to get stickers! Ads in the mags used to say to send a self-addressed stamped envelope—and in parenthesis, it would say 'SASE'—for free stickers."

"SASE," Mick says. "I haven't sent an SASE in ages."

"Send it! Send one."

"To who? To whom?"

"Moon Babes," Rodd says. "Moon Babes of Bicycle City."

"I'd send an SASE for a hat like Ukai's," Mick says. "A self-addressed stamped manila envelope. SASME with unmarked bills."

"She makes those hats herself."

"Rad. I'd wear a Moon Babes cycling cap."

"Cycling cap? You don't ride road bikes, O'Grady."

"Can I custom order a Moon Babes cycling cap? Like your dad's Life's a Beach one? Ukai?"

No response.

"Girl's like The Lizard King," Rodd says. "She can do anything. But you're, uh…you're missin' somethin'."

"What?"

"Somethin' important."

"What is it?"

"Stickers and patches are one thing, bike club gear is another."

"Huh?"

"Like I said on the road earlier: 'Moon Babes is a bike club like any other. You have to be asked to join. Chosen.'"

Ukai laughs. Continues reading the magazine.

"Remember zines?" Rodd asks. "Back when *Thrasher* was printed on newsprint, they reviewed 'skate rags' like *Squid Meat* and *Severe Head Injury*. They gave cities and states but not the addresses. If you couldn't figure out how to find 'em, then you weren't cool enough to read 'em. Were you gonna say somethin'?"

"I, uh, didn't know you skated, Rodderick."

"I didn't. I don't. I know you didn't either. Poser. I know you saw those articles in *Thrasher* though. I saw that interview you did on *FlatWebTV*. You started makin' *BMX Rag* zine for the Plywood Hoods Trick Team then you made *Aggro Rag Freestyle Mag!* You loved what you were doin' back then. You were such an enthusiast. Now everyone's a journalist. Mel Bend reviewed *Aggro Rag* in *Freestylin'* in what, '85? Or '86?"

"Right, Rodd."

"Well, homeboy, the bike club scene doesn't work quite like the zine scene did. Similar though. Somewhat similar."

"How similar?"

"Do you go to church, O'Grady?"

"Oh!" Mick says. "No!"

"'Church' is weekly meetings with your bike club."

"I knew that."

"That's as religious as it gets. Uncomfortable?"

"There was a bug on me."

"I just wanna ride," Rodd says.

"So do I," Mick says.

"We'll get to that. We'll get rad."

"I don't need another hat."

"Do you want one?"

"Yes."

"How about a vest?"

"Bullet-proof?"

"Denim."

"I had a feeling this was a gang."

Ukai laughs. Continues reading the BMX magazine.

"Team," Rodd says. "Moon Babes is a team effort. Bike club."

"Where's the rest of the bikes?"

"Warehouse. Follow me."

Chapter Five

Moon.
 Lady wearing jeans.
 Tight, faded jeans.
 Her legs are straight, she's bent at the waist, she's rummaging.
 Madon'!
 The checkerboard floor of Rodd's work space is strewn with bike boxes galore.
 A song is playing.
 Lady sings along with the lyrics.
 "O'Grady," Rodd says to Mick.
 The lady's rockin' Jox Jag sneakers from '81. Thom McAn.
 "O'Grady," Rodd repeats.
 The official shoe of Jag BMX.
 "O'GRADY!"
 She straightens and looks back at them.
 Hair curly like Cher's when Cher wondered if she could turn back time. Who is—?
 "Chatauqua?" Mick asks.
 "Chat, this is O'Grady," Rodd says. "Mick O'Grady from York, PA."
 "Hey O'Grady from York, PA! Chatauqua Moon from Atoka, OK."

Mick laughs.

She's wearing black Pacific Palms gloves and a Scorpions t-shirt. Vintage gear.

"Everybody calls me Chat. Well, not everybody. Most everybody."

"We just got back from the airport," Rodd says.

"It's a pleasure to meet you, Mrs. Moon."

"Likewise, Mick! You two must be hunger-pinched after travelin' all that way."

"We are," Rodd says.

"Were you chased?"

"We weren't."

"Chased?" Mick asks.

"No chase scenes," Rodd says. "Not yet."

"Mick needs a rental ride, I take it."

"He does. He wants to ride the Panda Pro-Am."

"R.C. Alderman's Panda! Excellent choice!"

"That's what I said to him."

"No, Rodd, I believe you said 'fantastic' as we passed Thrusters."

"Elina's Thrusters?" Chat asks. "Belly laugh. Why didn't you stop in for a bite, honey?"

"Parking lot was full o' choppers," Rodd says.

"Parking lot or the air?"

Rodd laughs.

It's 9:11 AM.

Under the digital clock on the far wall stands a white '99 Mat Hoffman Evel Knievel bike on the platform of a quarterpipe ramp.

Rows of rentals on both sides of the ramp.

"ACS banner," Mick says. "Is that from—?"

"Santee," Rodd says. "Yes it is. From the very first 2-Hip Meet the Street in Santee, Cali. ACS was one of the sponsors. I had to have that banner after the contest."

"Didn't Rich Bartlett do a wall ride and tear down one of

the banners?"
"He tried to, yeah. 'The Butcher'!"
"That was a crazy comp."
"Vander was there. Boss. Curb Dog."
"Rest in Peace."
"Who was that skinny speed metal kid who got the flat tire but he kept ridin'?" Chat asks.
"Jason Parkes," Rodd says.
"Jason Parkes, that's right. Jason was in his own world."
"Anyone wanna buy a Schwinn?" Rodd asks Mick. "Know anyone? We got a 5-Speed Grey Ghost up there for sale. Sting-Ray Krates are steady sellers for us but the Sting-Ray knock-offs from the '70s are way cooler to restore and ride all of a sudden. Bicentennial Edition Montgomery Ward Hawthornes. Montgomery Ward!"

Rodd presses "POWER" on a Zenith TV/VCR combo.

He opens a clamshell case and shakes out a videotape.

He holds up the tape for Mick to read:

HARDCORE	2-HIP 88 Series Video	ONE HOUR
BUT NOT	VHS 60 Minutes	OF
LOW-BUDGET		ACTION

"Pop this in here," Rodd says.
"I thought you guys were gonna go eat," Chat says.
"We are, Babe. Care for a bowl of Kix, O'Grady?"
"Oh, for sure. Kix?"

Mick says he recognizes Rodd's reference to *RAD: The Movie.* "Helltrack" in *RAD* had a cereal bowl with a Kix logo on it as one of the obstacles. The jump into the bowl was a piece of toast propped up on it. The jump out of the bowl was the handle of a spoon.

Rodd opens a cabinet door.

He takes out a box of Kix, two cereal bowls with *RAD* logos, two spoons.

He closes the cabinet.
Sets the bowls and spoons on a bike box.
Opens the Kix.
Pours.

Mick sees that the cabinet door has a *BMX Action* photo of Tony Murray blastin' air at Del Mar Skatepark taped to it.

Mick gets it, he says to Rodd.

"You get what?"

"Tony Murray on your cereal cabinet door. Tony the Tiger. Frosted Flakes."

Chat says she needs to get back to work.

Dorks.

Chapter Six

Chat has Wednesdays and Thursdays off so today—Friday—is her Monday, she says. That's why she's workin' and Rodderick isn't. In case Mick was wonderin'. Yesterday—Thursday—was his Friday. They're both workin' tomorrow though because of the contest, Chat reckons. They'll have a dealer display for Moon Babes. Facing Mick, she bends over and resumes packing a bike to ship. Chat goes on to say that the only days Rodd and her work together are Sundays, Mondays, and Tuesdays.

Rodd returns to the warehouse.

"Hey!"

"Here's your soy milk, O'Grady," Rodd says. "I forgot that you lived in L.A."

"San Fernando Valley mostly," Mick says.

"The Valley. My condolences. What did I miss?"

"Not too much, Mr. Moon. Thank you. It just started."

2-Hip videotape from '88.

Long shot of the first BMX street contest scene.

Parked in the foreground is a '76 Chrysler Cordoba.

Surrounding riders spray paint the Cordoba. The Cordoba.

Goldenrod with red and green.

The goldenrod matches the wall with ramps in the

background.

Mark Lewman—Lew—says into a micro-cassette recorder with a hot pink and black *Freestylin'* sticker on it that there's a whole lot of duct tape on the car. What does Dave Voelker have to say about that? Lew asks.

Dave says that's class. He's been thinkin' about doin' it to his truck.

Mad Dog rests on a race bike with black Tuffs and a number plate. Classicness.

A guy wearing a turquoise tank top tags a window.

Craig Grasso spray paints the trunk.

Pete Augustin fastplants off the corner.

R.L. Osborn lands on the hood. El Cid. He 270-hop-drops off.

Someone has written "VISION" and "GOD HELP US" across the windshield.

Its left front headlight is missing.

No side view mirrors.

A guy on a Kuwahara Bravo wall-rides the driver's side of the car. The Cordoba.

Pete Augustin sprocket-crunches the trunk.

Dave Voelker tells Lew that this has always been his favorite kind of ridin'—just ridin' on the street and stuff. And he's glad someone finally did somethin' about it, you know? Eddie Roman does a can can 360 to flat ground on the video.

"Oh!" Rodd bellows. "The Aggroman!"

The car and stuff, Dave goes on. It's somethin' you always dreamed of when you were out ridin' around. The way they set it up is rad. They came up with some good stuff like launch ramps over the car. Everything really, he says.

Craig Campbell—shirt tied to his handlebars—tries a

nose wheelie on the submarine box.
  A guy following him manuals the sub box.
  The video segment goes on.
  Rodd cheers at the end.
  "That 540 wall ride Campbell did was absolute lunacy!"
  "'Twas indeed," Mick says. "Ease-up, mate."
  TV is showing contest results for the "Good" class:

   GOOD

   VIC MURPHY
   SCOTT TOWNE
   MIKE GOLDEN
   RICH BARTLETT

The next screen continues:

   MARK ROLDAN
   TODD ANDERSON
   JAMES ARLINGTON
   GEORGE SMOOT

  The next screen shows results for the "Great" class:

   GREAT

   DAVE VOELKER
   CRAIG CAMPBELL
   R.L. OSBORN
   CRAIG GRASSO

MOON BABES OF BICYCLE CITY

Next screen:

> EDDIE ROMAN
> PETE AUGUSTIN
> DAVE VANDERSPEK
> RON WILKERSON

Rodd presses "STOP" on the TV's built-in VCR.
It's 9:27 AM.
Using his knee cap, he powers off the TV.
"Done reminiscin', gentlemen?" Chat asks.
"For a minute," Rodd says.
"After you wash those bowls, all these orders can go out."
"Aw," Mick says. "Did you pick up your room and make your bed this morning, Rodderick?"
"He got lucky today!" Chat says. "He went to bed early and got up before two to go pick you up at the airport."
"I just thought of something," Mick says.
"What is it?" Rodd asks.
"How did you pedal the bikecar from here to the airport all by yourself?"
Rodd and Chat look at each other.
Chat starts whistling.
She looks away.
Rodd looks at Mick.
"Name that tune, O'Grady."
"Who was with you? Who'd you drop off at the airport?"
"Name that tune."
"That your wife is whistling?"
"Name that tune."
"'With You' by John Farnham from the *RAD* soundtrack," Mick says. "The love theme."
"You got it! How did you get that?"
"Side two of the tape, second song."
"Tell him what he wins, Babe!"

Chat keeps whistling.

"Second or third song, I know it was side two. Greg Grubbs dubbed me a copy. Now will you answer my question?"

"Can you repeat the question?" Rodd asks.

"Who did you drop off at the airport?"

"I needed a little extra time to answer it, O'Grady."

"Huh?"

"He was a future business associate,[1] we'll leave it at that. Shall we?"

Chat stops whistling.

"Ride?" Mick asks.

Rodd nods.

"Give me a hand with these boxes first, will ya?"

"Yes sir."

---

[1] "I am hoping our mysterious stranger at the end of Chapter Six is a cartoonishly evil industrialist who uses Rodd to sell everyone out to monied automobile-driven interests, or a smugly evil land developer intent on using Bicycle City's character to draw in a flood of yuppie transplants who immediately begin eroding said character with their presence alone. If it's the latter, the worst thing about this villain is that he manages to be completely un-self-aware and still smugly self-satisfied at the same time."
—Shut-Ins

Chapter Seven

Babes.
    Customers.
    Contest-goers.
    Off-duty glassblowers. One's toting a blow torch. Maybe she's a welder.
    Business is brisk already.
    Bike rack outside holds a low rider, mountain climber, old school BMX freestyler, new school dirt jumper, two commuters, and a klunker with a *Fat Tire Flyer* sticker on the head tube.
    Young dude at the glass case counter.
    Probably 16 or so.
    He's wearing an acid washed denim vest.
    Top rocker on the back of his vest says:

    SCRAWNY FELLERS

    Embroidered design depicts a skeleton crouched down on a bike with aerodynamic fairing.
    Bottom rocker:

    LOCO HILLS

Ukai shows off a helmet with horns on it.

"No school today?" Mick asks Rodd.

He sets down a bike box. Moon Babes Retire Bikes logo on it.

"College is closed as you can see by the betties with the suntanned legs," Rodd says. "Repop your eyes back in your head, buddy. No school Monday either."

Bronzed gams.

Babes are babes but not all babes are Moon Babes, Mick thinks. Moon Babes of Bicycle City.

> Moon Babes
>   Forever
>   Forever
> Moon Babes

Mick could see that on a patch.

How many are there of these Moon Babes? he wonders. How many chapters?

Laughter.

College girls.

Devil-horned helmet.

Chat is ringing up a digital camouflage wheelbarrow. The purchaser tells her he's from Pittsburgh. He's here for

business and laughs.
Business and laughs! Chat says. Good combination! She likes that.
Might as well pick up a pair of these Odyssey gloves too, the customer says. He'll need 'em for diggin'.
Hot dayum, Mick thinks regarding Chat. Rodderick's one lucky man. Babes are babes but not all babes are Moon Babes. Moon Babe #1, Chatauqua Moon.
Everyone calls her Chat.
Except the fixter Rodd had mentioned earlier. Total poser on the Milwaukee Bruiser.
Mick sees a framed magazine page photo of Chat taken 30 years ago when she raced BMX for Jag.
Catchin' some *air*.
She wore Vera leathers.
Or were they BW pants? Bill Walters?
Mick can't tell what kind they were.
Photo was taken from behind.
Back of her leathers says:

    MOON
      BABE

Strange thinking Chat and Rodd were teenage sweethearts. She had "Farrah Fawcett Hair" but brunette instead of blonde and she wore lip gloss, he sees from the circular inset pic—
"Excuse me, brotha."
Odyssey gloves in his wheelbarrow. Biceps. The guy from Pittsburgh. He's grinning.
Mick opens the door for him.
"I like that shirt, man. The rapper P.O.S?"
"Yeah!" Mick says
"Doomtree!"
"Yeah man."

"Doomtree Records in Minneapolis, Minnesota."
"Yeah!" Mick says. "Or in my case, CDs."
"What is goin' on here?" Rodd asks.
"Jewel cases," Mick says. "I just made a passing reference to jewel cases. And digipaks."
"We gotta get you out of here, O'Grady."
Store is crowded.
Rodd leads Mick back to the warehouse.
Sign over the doors says:

SHOP

"I like that," Mick says. "SHOP."

Chapter Eight

No moon this time.
   Mick can focus more.
   Kix took the edge off.
   He shuts off the faucet.
   He sets the second bowl upside down on the drying rack.
   "Ready for radness," Mick says. "Rodderick?"
   Rodderick wheels in the chrome Panda Pro-Am. Perfect timing. Almost too perfect. Red Line V-Bars. Red ACS Z Rims. Black knobbies. Red vinyl pad set with snaps.
   "That's incredible!" Mick says. "R.C. Alderman rode front brakes?"
   "Yeah, he did."
   "He must have read 'Harry Leary's Front Brake Secrets' in *Bicycle Motocross Action* then—October '81, Volume 6, Number 10, page 90."
   "Down to the page number!" Rodd says. "That is downright frightening. When you get a chance, check that ACS ad again where Alderman tacos his Z Rim. He ran Dia-Compe alloy two-finger levers like Haro Handles."
   "Panda actually made a double top tube frame back in '78," Mick says.
   "The Panda Elite, I'm aware. It came in nickel-plated like Pattersons and Jags did. And powder epoxy baked white.

No known survivors."

"Cannot stump you, can I Old Sport? You are on it."

"And you, my friend, are about to be on this classic Panda from Concord, California! Once you sign our waiver."

"Where do I sign?" Mick asks. "Where's the dotted line?"

"It's not dotted but right there. Here's a pen."

It's a Moon Babes of Bicycle City ballpoint pen.

Mick clicks it open. He signs.

"And your signature there."

He signs.

"Initials there."

Mick initials it: M.O'G.

"And there."

Initials.

Staring at Rodd, Mick clicks the pen closed and pockets it.

"Aren't you wonderin' what I'm gonna be ridin'?" Rodd asks.

"What rig are you gonna be ridin'?"

"It'll be my maiden voyage on it."

"What is it?"

"It's burly."

"The Hoffman that looks like Evel's Harley?"

"Not that burly. Same era as the Pro-Am. Can you say 'era correct'? Is that even in your vocabulary?"

Mick gives up, he says.

"It's something you'd never expect, O'Grady. It's gonna blow your mind. I'll give you a hint."

"Go for it."

"The hint'll give it away, but that's OK because we got some roastin' to do. It's almost ten o'clock already."

"OK. What's the hint?"

"'Bio-Air.'"

"Oh. My. God."

"Steve 'Bio-Air' Bennett."

"Are you kidding?"

"My rendition of the GJS that Steve Bennett ripped on at Skate City in Whittier. Yes! The bike's companion piece is an '82 G&S Neil Blender 'Jumper' skateboard—Blender's second pro deck—because according to a photo caption in *BMX Action*, Neil Blender saw Bennett's 'insane oververtical style of re-entry' in the pool and he christened it—"

"'Bio-Air,'" Mick says. "Bring it. The bike."

"Be right back with it. Keep in mind that I can't be held responsible for damage that occurs when your chin hits the cement."

"Oh, I understand. I saw that clause in the fine print."

Rodd walks off to get the bike.

Mick picks up a deck of Donruss BMX trading cards. Copyright says 1984. He riffle-shuffles the cards. Does a one-handed fan flourish. He looks at the fanned cards, now the other side. He returns the cards to stacked formation.

"I heard that!" Rodd calls out. "No gamblin'!"

Mick sits on an SE Racing canvas chair.

He meditates for a moment.

Hears something.

He opens his eyes. Bio-Air. GJS A-Frame. Bottema forks. Bowed-out black Series One number plate. Blue Comp ST tires.

Rodd has changed his shirt to a *BMXA* jersey with purple raglan sleeves.

He's put on yellow, black, and white Max pants and red elbow pads.

He must have had to change his sneakers for era-correctness, Mick thinks. Checkered Vans now.

Red ankle guards.

The Swatches are gone from his wrist.

Yellow Premier open face helmet held by the chin strap. Red visor. Black Max rub-on sticker on it, upside down.

"We treasure our past in Bicycle City," Rodd says. "But

we celebrate the present by actually riding our relics. The terrain we've cultivated endangers ourselves and our fellow citizens. And our visitors. We're very passionate about that."

"I see," says Mick. "I'd like to see more."

"Gear up. Dressing room's in the back."

Chapter Nine

Mick changes his P.O.S t-shirt to a Radio Concuss to match the bike.

Black, red, and white.

So he won't have to switch out the DOOM Dunk Nikes he's wearin'.

Nike SPR VLN's.

Collector's items.

Back when they were still in the box.

He customized 'em with the Aesop Rock round laces.

Grey jeans he's got on are keepin' the knobby knees undercover.

Kids would ask Mick during summers in York why wasn't he wearin' shorts? Was he crazy? In this heat? And high humidity?

Legs are too skinny.

His response could've been that easy.

R.L. Osborn didn't wear shorts very often either.

Not unless he was lake jumpin'.

Even when he *was* lake jumpin', now that Mick thinks of it.

R.L. was wearin' jeans when he did that 360 off the dock into the lake at the end of the Mountain Dew commercial.

Mick puts on his Bell helmet and Atmosphere fingerless

gloves.

He zips shut his backpack.

No, he reconsiders. It's too hot for these.

He takes off the gloves.

He unzips the backpack, stows the gloves, zips it shut.

This is startin' to make some sense.

Mick picks it up.

He opens the dressing room door and exits.

Paramedics.

Rodd's got a Trek Y-33 mountain bike up on a repair stand.

"Pronounced pain, O'Grady!" he calls out.

The paramedics laugh.

Female, male.

"I failed to mention I'm a certified suspension technician," Rodd says to the female paramedic. "Check your oil, m'am?"

He drums his fingers on the red Stratos Pro rear shock.

"Yes," she says. "Please."

Is her tongue pierced? Mick wonders. Slight lisp.

"Hi, I'm Mick," he says to her.

"Glorieta," she says.

Unpierced tongue, Mick sees.

"Nice to meet you, Glorieta. And you must be—?"

"Angelo," the male paramedic says.

Angelo and Mick shake hands.

"Mick's visitin' from Oregon," Rodd says. "Hopefully you won't be seein' too much of him. I know I will."

"Our panniers come from Portland, Oregon," Angelo says.

"'Pan-yers'," Mick says. "I was wonderin' how you pronounced those saddle bags on the sides."

"Panniers," Glorieta says. "Yes."

"Custom made for NMM," Angelo says. "New Mexico Medics."

"I can have your overhaul done next Monday, Glorieta," Rodd says. "Gotta order some parts."

"October the 14th?"
"Not this Monday. Next Monday. The, uh…"
"Better check his calendar!" Angelo says and laughs.
Rodd checks his Carpet Queens calendar.
"October 21st," Rodd says.
"OK," Glorieta says. "I guess. I'll ride my Yeti."
"You've been hammerin' hardcore on this thing. That's what I like to see."
Emergency call comes in on a walkie-talkie or two-way radio. Glorieta responds. Angelo says later guys. They leave the warehouse.
"Careful everybody!" Rodd calls out after them.

It's 9:56 AM.

Mick says he saw that Rodd checked his Carpet Queens calendar. Miss October looks pretty serious about her Petersons in front of a roaring fire. Is that a Skyway T/A?

"Good eye, O'Grady."

"Totally tricked out," Mick says. "She even has a Mickey Mouse bell on her bars like 'The Master of Balance' Robert Peterson had. How badass."

"Ground Control Freestyle Team from Foster City represent!"

"Is that where Carpet Queens are from?" Mick asks. "San Francisco?"

"New York. They're based in Queens, New York."

"Carpet Queens Bike Club is from Queens. That makes total sense almost."

"Carpet Queens are BMX society's 'One Percenters,'" Rodd says.

"BMXSociety.com?"

"No, BMX society in general. Social misfits to begin with, you know? Carpet Queens are the elite one percent of us who've managed to become independently wealthy social misfits. The Dons who can afford anything. They ransack old school bike shop owners' garages and basements and attics. Or their men do. Women accomplices."

"Ooh," Mick says.

"From coast to coast, they're relentless," Rodd goes on. "Their ruthlessness to expand their collections is second to none. Step One: Negotiate. Step Two: Liquidate. Carpet Queens have cleaned out entire warehouses that way. It's insane. It's sick but they're smart. Any bike or part or article of clothing they want, they get it and they keep it stored in the original packaging."

"NOS," Mick says. "'New Old Stock.'"

"NOS. Yeah. Until they build their ultimate showpiece or they don't want it anymore or until they want somethin' else they see online of course, then they flip it. That's why dudes call it the mentally-illest bike club on the planet."

"Because they're jealous?"

"They flip or they trade. I've worked out a few trades here and there but it's very rare. I got lucky. Jealous? Did you say?"

"Yes," Mick says. "I am. Do they call Carpet Queens the mentally-illest bike club on the planet because they're so envious of their collections?"

Rodd puts on his helmet.

"They're green with envy. Neon green with envy. The calendar models ride more than the Dons do. That's the sickest thing about 'em."

"That is one stretched Peterson she's doin', I must say. Stretched-to-the-max."

"Oh, they get into it," Rodd says. "The models do actual freestyle tricks. The first year they did the calendar—2010, I think—the girls were just posin' with the bikes. Which, by the way, not all of 'em were the freshest. Some of 'em were so ridiculously overbuilt, they were obscene."

"The models?"

"The bikes," Rodd says. "The show bikes."

"Oh, I thought you meant the calendar ladies."

"No, the bikes. Some of Carpet Queens' first builds were such tragedies. Catastrophes. Eye candy shenanigans."

"Dio*ny*sian Crankensteins," Mick says. "The 'NY' in 'Dionysian' needs to be capitalized on their hats to stand for 'New York': DioNYsian's Crankensteins."

"Neck bolts sold separately," Rodd says.

Mick laughs.

"They have to color-coordinate everything. Araya triple-dipped chrome rims with black and red anodized spoke nipples. Who had set-ups like that, O'Grady? No one that I ever saw. They pick the most expensive cranksets you could get from mail order ads in the mags or catalogs. Titron titanium pedals with high-polished LRP cages? Remember LRP? Loncarevich Racing Products? I could keep goin'."

"Go on."

"We gotta get ridin'."

"Oh yeah."

"I want you to see somethin' first on this GJS. Scope the treads on these tires. They still have the release powder showin' on 'em. That is straight from the Tioga factory, babycakes. Mid-'80s."

"OMG. Seriously."

Mick takes out his phone. He taps the camera app. Takes a close-up photo of the back tire. Asks Rodd why he's doin' this.

Rodd snaps on his yellow Jofa mouthguard.

"Why am I doin' what?"

"Why are you gonna *ride* your '82 Steve Bennett 'Bio-Air' GJS? Shouldn't it be in a showcase in a climate-controlled museum? Next to Pat Benatar's guitar?"

"Neil Giraldo was Pat's lead guitarist. She didn't play. She married him. Well, I guess you could ask my wife Chat that question: 'Why did Rodd decide to ride his Bio-Air?' She'll have a more in-depth answer to it. Since she's also my psycho-analyst. But I'll tell you this, man. I'll tell you this. I don't know what's gonna happen, man, but I wanna get my kicks before—"

"Kix? You just had a bowl of Kix."

Rodd laughs.

"Time to ride, O'G. Leave your backpack. Lock it in that locker. Take the key."

Chapter X

NM.
  New Mexico.
  Crescit eundo.
  "It grows as it goes."
  The original Sunshine State.
  Land of Enchantment.
  Land of Embankments...
  Bicycle City, New Mexico.
  Even the bingo hall has a bank-to-wall.
  And a hip.
  Two ladies on a Jamis Earth Cruiser commuter. Aqua on plum purple. Ubiquitous milk crate serving as the basket.
  Stack of records in the crate and a stuffed animal.
  Oh, it's Road Runner—stuffed bird.
  Stuffed cartoon bird.
  When did axle pegs become "passenger foot rests"? Mick wonders as he watches.
  Somewhere he saw pegs described like that.
  Must not have been a safety manual.
  The lady on the back tickles the armpits of the rider. Makes her laugh.
  Says something in her ear.
  Or she's singing.

They must be going shopping.
Digging for vinyl.
A column of Spinal Health Associates riding restored pre-War Excelsiors passes them.
Rodd says to Mick, "Do a trick."
"Thank you Woody Itson!" says Mick. Give him a second, he has to think of one he can do on this thing. He's still gettin' used to it. Horrendous headwind. He stands up on the pedals. "Alright," he says. "So it won't be a 180 rollback because of the wind. Let's go for a 360 bunnyhop, shall we? 'Mike Buff-on-a-Quadangle-in-the-Taco Bell-parking lot' style from *BMX Action*."
Mick bunnyhops 180. He lands the Panda on the back tire and the nylon Z Rim flexes. Mick struggles to bring the front end around. Hissing.
Flat tire.
Son of a crop duster.
Less than ten minutes from the shop.
Exactly why Mick never had Zytel plastic rims. His brother did though—yellow ones on a chrome Torker. He had an Addicks nylon chainring that matched the rims.
Rodd already has a patch kit in the palm of his MXL-gloved hand.
Rodd undoes the quick release on the belt of his hip pack. He puts the patch kit in the hip pack. Zips it shut. Hands the hip pack to Mick.
"Fix that flat."
"Go on without me, Rodd."
"No. I can't leave you here."
"Why not?"
"There's a search underway for a missing man. One is enough. Don't be a fool, O'Grady. Search teams are scouring the canyons and mountainsides as we speak."
"I'm already wide-eyed in the wilds."
Rodd laughs.

"You need an ice cold canyon of Frail Sisters coffee," Rodd says. "That'll widen your eyes as you fix that flat."

"Bitchen, brother! Black, please. Unsweetened."

"Patch it up enough for us to roll back to the shop. You can exchange it for something else that tickles your fancy. Whatever other set-up you wanna ride. You said you saw our Fall catalog. I forgot how problematic those rims are when you taco 'em. Spoke nipples poke through the tubes. I'll hit up this Allsup's Market for refreshments."

Tickles, Mick thinks.

Those ladies a few minutes ago. The one tickling the other's armpits.

All felt so well then. Now this. Fix.

Bicycles have problems.

Real problems sometimes.

Easy to forget that fact sometimes, he guesses.

Mick unscrews the red and white dice cap from the valve stem of the tube.

Rad Kaps.

He places it upside down on the desert.

Die.

Singular for "dice" is "die".

He checks the sky for circling birds.

None that he can see.

Sun is blazing.

Mick presses his thumbnail into the valve and releases more air.

He unseats the tire bead from the right side of the Z Rim. Begins removing the tube. This would be so much easier with the back wheel off.

He squeezes the Dia-Compe MX-1000 brake arms. Using his right thumb and pointer finger, he pulls the quick release lever down and flips it counter-clockwise. Lets go.

The caliper widens.

He unzips the hip pack and empties it of its contents:

patch kit, pump, wrench, socket, stack of stickers for the contest tomorrow. What are these? The keys to Rodd's bikecar replica of the '76 Chrysler Cordoba.

Not very "era-correct" of Rodderick to be wearing a hip pack while riding a GJS, Mick thinks. He flattens it on the ground to protect the red Kashimax seat. Made in Japan.

He flips the Panda onto its seat and the red Oakley .5 grips with the black Mud 'n Crud plugs.

He picks up the wrench and fits the socket onto the non-drive-side axle nut.

He loosens the axle nut, ratchets, loosens, ratchets, loosens.

He loosens the other one, ratchets, loosens, ratchets, loosens.

He pushes the axle forward, derails the chain, disengages the wheel.

Removes the inner tube from the tire casing.

He picks up the pump and hooks it onto the valve.

"Flat-out hookin' it on!" Mick says.

He inflates the tube. Listens for air escaping. Finds the hole. Holes? Hole.

This shouldn't be so difficult, Mick thinks.

Really.

He can do this.

He picks up the patch kit and opens the lid of the container. A piece of sandpaper blows out.

It's grip tape.

He picks it up. Uses it to abrade the area around the hole.

He returns the grip tape to the patch kit.

Mick takes out the tube of glue and unscrews the cap. He applies three drops to the sanded area. One for each of Rodd and Chat's daughters: Suzue, Araya, and Ukai Moon. Named after the hub and rim makers in Japan.

He evenly distributes the glue using the nozzle tip of the tube.

MOON BABES OF BICYCLE CITY

He re-caps the tube and puts it back in the patch kit.
Where is their dad with that ice cold coffee?
Mick remembers hearing that New Mexico moved up and down an inch after that earthquake in Japan.
Japan's 9.0 magnitude earthquake in 2011.
He heard about it on the radio.
2011, worst year of his life.
Most fortunate though, now that he thinks of it.
One that had to happen to be where he is right now.
But what makes now so great? Well, he is off work for an extended weekend on vacation in Bicycle City, New Mexico. There's that.
This.
Not at the time did 2011 feel like the most fortunate year of his life though. Hell. 2015 then.
People have problems.
Real problems sometimes.
Easy to forget that fact sometimes.
Here he is now in 2019 however.
Friday, October 11th.
Mick peels the wrap off an inner tube patch.
Bicycle City is busy.
Hearing cheerfulness from riders passing gladdens him.
Tires hum past on macadam and the gravel. The sand.
Music from sounds of bike chains and the howling. Wind.
The round patch says on it:

   MOON
   BABES

He presses down with his thumb.
Holds it in place.
Wonders.

MOON BABES OF BICYCLE CITY

MOON
BABES

Wonders about them.

MOON
BABES

Chapter Eleven

Rodd waves at a boulder that resembles a Bell Moto III helmet. Digital eyes behind the goggles follow them as they pass. Mick thinks it must be an interactive 3D billboard ad or something, he hopes. He sips from the can of Frail Sisters XXX coffee that Rodd got him.

"You know Adrianna Pennino?" Mick asks.

"No. Why? Should I? Who is she?"

"Adrianna Pennino-Balboa."

"Who?"

"Mrs. Rocky Balboa."

"Oh," Rodd says. "'Yo Adrian!'"

"Adrian was played by Talia Shire who played Cru Jones' mom in *RAD*," Mick says. "Did you know that Bill Allen—our pal the actor who played Cru Jones in *RAD*—was in *Breaking Bad*?"

"He was?"

"Yeah. Bill was in Season One. The episode was called 'Gray Matter.' He played a scientist named William Allen. He's in the scene where Walt and Skyler go to Elliott Schwartz's birthday party."

"Did he have a speaking part?"

"Yeah. He talked with Walter White. Heisenberg!"

"I know they filmed that show up in Albuquerque," Rodd

says. "*Breaking Bad.*"

Speaking of Sylvester Stallone who played Rocky, Mick says he was thinking about something while he was fixing that flat earlier. "Yo!" is another way to say "Hey!" or "Hello!" It doesn't have to be to someone he knows though. He could just be being a friendly fellow. Mick laughs. They're pedaling along here on this bike path, for example. Back to the lab. What if he needs to get someone's attention? He could call it out—"Yo!"—and prevent an accident from happening. So many brakeless bikes and ear buds these days. Or maybe some dudes will call it out to *them* with news about a session that's going down—somewhere they didn't hear about because it wasn't planned, it just happened. Total jam. And Mick hopes something eventful does happen soon, yo.

"Danger lies ahead," Rodd says. "Don't you worry, O'Grady."

Mick says he stopped saying that at the ends of sentences for emphasis. Yo. He caught himself saying it seven years ago. And it wasn't because that's when he rented *Jackass Presents: Mat Hoffman's Tribute to Evel Knievel* and "The Condor" himself said it to cap off a couple lines. Yo. No. It was a bad habit that he got into for some other reason.

"Go on," Rodd says.

Oh, now Mick remembers how he got into it. He dated a lady who rode a Phat Kaddy Cruiser De Ville. It had "ape drapes" handlebars and leather grips like a Harley. She said it at the ends of sentences. Yo. Nothin' happened between them though. It didn't get that far.

"That's too bad."

But they did ride together on several occasions that summer, Mick goes on. In Portland, Oregon. Biking's big in the Pacific Northwest, Rodd might've heard. Does he get out much?

"No."

Neither does Mick really. He readily admits.

"At least a tailwind is blowin' in the direction we're goin'," Rodd says. "That's always nice."

"Nice."

He nods to a guy with an eye patch and a black and tan backpack as they pass.

No response.

"That dude with the eye patch," Rodd says. "Cruisin' the department store mountain bike he had spray painted all flat black. I think he's from Minneapolis. You never see dudes like that ridin' in packs. Ever. They're always rollin' solo non-stop unless cops are chasin' 'em and they're about to get tackled. Another reason why they're always wearin' long sleeves. They don't join bike clubs. A part of me admires that though, you know what I mean? True independent spirits. Tireless outlaws, so to speak. Lone rangers. Free agents. They have flexible schedules. An Old Southwestern saying goes, 'As long as a man is willin' to work, he'll come out all right.' Occasionally I hire 'em for odd jobs."

Mick drains the grainy dregs of the Frail Sisters coffee.

He dunks the can into a bin with three arrows flowing in a circle.

"That was for hazardous materials, wasn't it?" Mick asks.

Rodd laughs.

He looks Mick in the eyes and throws a handful of stickers over his shoulder.

The stickers scatter.

Flutter.

Rodd says something. Mutters.

"What?" Mick asks. "I didn't hear you what you said."

"Here comes Gene."

"Who?"

"Genevieve Fennelseed."

"Oh. Yeah. Jean."

Ginger on a front-loader cargo bike hauling a trailer.

Lipstick lady. She's wearing a bandana headband. Tank top. Cuffed capri jeans. Converse.
　She waves.
　Hairy armpit! Ooh...
　"Moon!" she calls out.
　Tongue lolling.
　She exaggerates reckless steering.
　Elderly man on a boneshaker beeps as he's overtaken.
　She blows a kiss back to him. Laughs. Lolling.
　"Mister Moon Maaannnnn!"
　Fist up.
　Gonzo.
　Reconnaissance woman. Tatted-up arms and shins. Neck. So *this* is Gen—
　"Jean!" Rodd calls out. "Meet Mick O'Grady."
　"Hey O'Grady!"
　She grabs both brake levers. Slows to a stop. Knocks her fists together. Holds the pose. Pouts. Knuckle tattoos:

　　STUN SEED

　"'STUN SEED'?" Rodd reads.
　"Did it with a Sharpie."
　"Ridiculous."
　"Hi. I'm Mick."
　"Welcome to the city, Mick! I know you as 'O'Grady' from stories I heard when we were workin' on Moon Man's bikecar."
　"I heard you're hard to find sometimes."
　"I'm just plain hard."
　"I'd shake your hand but my right arm is spasming."
　"Chronic condition he has," Rodd says.
　"I got a flat tire already," Mick says.
　"We're on our way back to the shop so O'Grady can get a different rider."

"One that's dialed in a little better hopefully," Mick says.

"I was just there," Jean says. "Major shred session goin' down on your bikecar."

"What?" Rodd asks.

"Hesher was hoppin' on the hood."

Rodd takes a deep breath. Exhales.

He reattaches the Jofa mouthguard.

Reaches down. Positions his right crank arm exactly two freewheel clicks above level. He stands up on the pedals. Shimano SX, if Mick isn't mistaken.

Rodd balances for a moment. Snaps from the stance. He sprints. Power wheelie now like he's speed jumping whoop de doos...

Jean looks at Mick.

"Oh boy."

Chapter Twelve

Genevieve Fennelseed tells Mick she has somewhere to be for lunch. She'll meet him and Moon Man later at that ghetto snake run made out of pallets and plywood. She'll bring marshmallows to toast. And her tea. And her girlfriend. And the back seat cover she quilted for the bikecar. She said the marshmallows are vegan.

Eye-arrestin' appeal, that "Genie" Fennelseed.

She's the same age as him and Rodd probably.

Fifty.

Anarchy, Odyssey, Rocket from the Crypt, Dessert is for Lovers, and other stickers cover the flatbed of her Surly trailer. Also "BC" for "Bicycle City," the New Mexico state flag, *Urban Velo*, Tabletop Tavern, Lazy Fascist.

Glue residue on Mick's fingertips and grips from the patch kit.

A gathering is happening at the Moon Babes establishment with Public Address system announcing. Moon Babes Retire Bikes. Oh, no. It's Rodderick on his MTV microphone. He's standing beside the Cordoba bikecar. Blathering. Now he's whispering. Whatever it was has the crowd laughing. And a cameraman smiling. And the host of a show. Holy Shimano! Is that Rick?

Thorne?

Snapback hat worn backwards with a flat brim, that's him. The Biker in Black. Microphone and a can of Monster. The Biker in Black. Long shorts, STAY RAD sleeveless, sweatbands on his wrists. The Biker in Black. He's in a band called Good Guys in Black. The one he was in before that was called Rick Thorne.

Rodd Moon and Rick Thorne aren't the only cyclists in uniform, Mick notices. Mountain biker in Lycra on a green Santa Cruz Heckler. Dude wearing MF Dyno gear on a yellow Fiola PROFORMER. Sorority sister on a red Tourney Free Spirit 10-speed. Rasta trifecta. Random.

Short shorts bonanza.

Mick stops his Panda next to a woman and a man wearing matching pajamas on a royal blue Pegasus tandem.

Kick turn ramp braced against the passenger side door of the Cordoba bikecar.

A man on a blue CW with black Tuffs does a Dizz Hicks "Maiden Power Pivot" kick turn. He stretches it. Sticks it. Must be the hasher, Mick thinks. The hesher.

"Whoa!" Rodd says over the Cordoba's loudspeaker. "Coaster brake mayhem on the wedge! OK, so what do you get when you mix Chili Peppers, Rollins, Rage, Tupac, Sinatra, Beastie Boys, and screamo? But not screamo emo? Give up? Yo! *Never* give up! Rick Thorne! Right here at our shop! Make some noise!"

"Yeah!" Mick cheers.

Rick laughs. His reporter-style microphone has a skull and crossbones on it. What he's saying isn't amplified because it's for an episode of a show. Video edit for the Internet. He walks toward Rodd. Rick's cameraman follows. The cameraman is seated on a chrome Haro Master Cruiser. Rolling. Still smiling. Rick seems to be inquiring about the Cordoba.

Rodd tells Rick that the framework was custom made by Bandito in Corona. Under the hood are two sets of Cook cranks. No electric assistance whatsoever, he says. It does happen to have power windows and A/C, however. The prototype bikecar had Peregrine Madd Max 48-spoked rims on it, but now it's got white Skyway Tuff Wheel II mags with stadium tires courtesy of Tioga.

"Where's the pegs?" Rick asks.

Rodd appears stunned for a moment.

He hadn't thought of puttin' on pegs, he must confess. He'll have to get some axle extenders on it pronto for the contest tomorrow. Now that Ricardo's mentioned it, it's gotta have pegs. Steel pegs, not aluminum or nylon. Thank you Ricardo Montalbán!

"Don't mention it, buddy!" Rick says. "Ha! Montalbán? He wore all white though, didn't he? On *Fantasy Island*? With Tattoo? Hey listen man, we gotta keep movin' so we'll talk to you soon. Alright? Yo, Rodd Moon everybody! Stay Rad."

The Biker in Black walks on.

Cameraman follows him. Rolling.

"I've got some boltin' on to do," Rodd says to Mick. "Stat!"

"It's been said that bolt-on is better," Mick says. "I think I read that in a GT ad."

Hesher hits the kick turn ramp again. Candybar nutcracker in Jordache jeans. Awesome brand hi-top sneakers. Coaster brake fakie rollback.

He pulls it.

Rodd opens the driver side door and returns the microphone to the center console.

He slams the door. Locks it with key.

"Warehouse, O'Grady. Follow me."

Chapter Thirteen

History lesson Mick wasn't expecting.
 Regarding cars ridden on at BMX street contests.
 Written on and then ridden on with the spray paint still wet.
 Rodd'll never forget that Caddy they destroyed in La Jolla. So rad.
 Mick couldn't go to that contest. He saw coverage of it in the mags though. And on the videos.
 Rodd says it was a '75 Cadillac Seville. Parked smack-dab in the center of the course with ramps set up everywhere. Mark Eaton was there. He was ridin' for Trend Bike Source, Rodd thinks. "Lungmustard" and Kevin Jones from York. The Plywood Hoods! Campbell won the Great class. Dyrenforth won Good. Contest was so crazy with the road bike race happenin' that same weekend—the La Jolla Grand Prix or whatever. Rodd and Chat were there with their newborn baby, Araya. Suzue was there, too. She was three. Almost three.
 "How old is Suzue now?" Mick asks.
 "Do the math!" Rodd says. "Here's some scratch paper."
 Rodd hands a flyer to Mick.
 It's a 2-Hip contest flyer dated April 16, 1989.
 Mick flips over the flyer. It's folded in thirds. He pulls

the pen from the back pocket of his jeans.

MOON BABES OF BICYCLE CITY

That won't be necessary, Rodd says to him. He takes back the flyer. Suzue just turned 30. He refolds the flyer and returns it to its envelope.

"So wait," Mick says. "You were...what? Twenty? When you became a dad?"

"Nineteen."

"How old was Chat?"

"What is this? An interview now? Eighteen."

"Teenage sweethearts?"

"Somethin' like that. Sure, O'Grady. So what's your story?"

"I've been trying to figure that out."

Rodd laughs. "Go on."

"Go on," Mick says. "That's what I keep telling myself. Take out the space and it says 'goon'. Go on, goon."

Rodd says he knows for sure that the third contest car was a Ford Granada. Probably a 1980 Four-Door Ghia Sedan. He couldn't make it out to that one.

"Where were you that was more important than Woodward, PA, May '89?"

"Hospital room in Davis."

"Where?"

"Hospital care."

"For what?"

"Separated shoulder."

"Bar fight?"

"Road bike. Train tracks after midnight."

"Might I ask why a road bike? Never mind."

"Transportation. Up until that happened, my Raleigh was gettin' me home from the alfalfa mill faster than my CycleCraft even."

"So your 'Kevin Bacon from the movie *Quicksilver*

impersonation' was a short-lived phase you went through then, I take it?"

"Nostalgia hurts."

Mick laughs. "Poignant statement. Nostalgia hurts. Now we're gettin' somewhere."

"Talkin' about ridin' when we should be out ridin'?"

"I agree," Mick says. "I hereby hand over the Panda with my deepest apologies to R.C. Alderman and the establishment. And ACS, American Cycle System."

What can Rodd get Mick on instead? Rodd asks him.

Mick is scrolling through the PDF catalog. "One moment please. The Mongoose. Mongoose Supergoose."

With or without Oakley 3 grips?

"Without."

Rodd'll be right back with it. Cut to a commercial, O'Grady.

Mick crosses the warehouse to an arcade game, *Joust*. Knights riding flying ostriches. Their enemies ride buzzards. Williams Electronics, Inc. He feels in his pocket for the quarter he got in change at the airport this morning. He finds the coin. Inserts it into the machine. Presses the "START" button. Moves the joystick. The ostrich runs. He stops it from running. Flaps. He's flying.

Rodd reappears, Mick hears. Mick asks Rodd if he remembers the Mongoose ad that said, "Who says, 'man can't fly'." Two-page spread with Jeff Kosmala catchin' air off a jump in the mountains. "The Kos" from Team Mongoose. No response. Mick glances from the video game screen. "Why the thousand-yard stare?" he asks Rodd. "And the dropped jaw? Where's the Supergoose I ordered?"

Pause. Long pause.

"We've been robbed."

Chapter Fourteen

All Rodd's got left is the Supergoose with the Bullwinkle grips—the Oakley 3's—is what he meant to say. Sorry for not updatin' the catalog. Rodd forgot that he rented the other one to a little old lady who wanted a Sunday for her grandson and the Supergoose for her son.

Mick jousts a knight off his buzzard. The knight turns into an egg that lands on a floating rock platform. Mick lands his ostrich and runs it over the egg. Seven hundred and fifty points.

Horn that sounds like a trumpet blast.

Forklift bike bursts through the warehouse doors.

Babe.

"Yowza," Mick says.

"I say that at the end of every Guns N' Roses song," Rodd says. "'Yowza.' Seems your game is over."

"So I hear," Mick says. "So it goes."

"Well if it isn't Miss 'To Be Continued!'" Rodd calls out.

"What did you just call me?" the forklift bike operator asks. She lowers a pallet of boxes. Looks at Mick. Blue don't-give-a-damn eyes. Black hair in a bun. PINK tank top and long shorts. Tattoos. Silver-glittered Doc Martens. "Who's the hang around?" she asks.

"Hi. I'm Mick."

"Epiphany."

Septum nose piercing.

Bubblegum-chewing babe.

Hand in his pocket, "rooting for a quarter" he'd like to be regarded as doing, Mick finds one. He inserts it into the machine.

"There's a tallbike joust at that frat boy roof ball kegger," Epiphany says. "I had to leave before someone got hurt bad."

"Are we secured for the space?" Rodd asks her.

"Space is secured."

"Area with the fire hydrant?"

"Yes. And it's been checked. It works. Hooraw."

"Hooraw Plaza," Rodd says. "Well done, Noctchaw. Hear that, O'Grady?"

"Epiphany Noctchaw?"

"We got the space we need for the SFR street course tomorrow!"

"Strange Famous Records?" Mick asks. "Really?"

"Southern Frontier Relics," Rodd says. "Chuck wagon box jump with double-barrel grind rails. Quarterpipes cobbled together with old merchant signs. Miner shack kick turn ramps. Rust is good traction. Vintage barbed wire fences—"

"The barbed wire was my idea," Epiphany Noctchaw says.

"Ultra gnarly," Mick says. "I love it. Go on, goon."

"Do not—I repeat, do *not* miss the Opening Ceremony, O'Grady."

"He will. Slacker."

Mick smiles. Looks at Epiphany Noctchaw. How does she know?

"Wild Style Graffiti Demo," Rodd continues. "Street riders and bikini babes will be spray bombin' the BikeCardoba. Chat'll have the five-foot-high adobe bread oven mogul fired up for buckwheat scones and bizcochitos cookies. And Fennelseed's blue corn tortillas and veggie fajitas—"

"Yeah!" Mick cheers.

"What else will there be? Oh, our launch ramps layered with remaindered BMX mags from the past 10 years. Front tires will be washin' out left and right on those. We test-rode the ramps and they shred! Watch out for the staples."

"Staples? No, please. Not staples."

"All staples intact."

"Ever hear of a staple remover?" Mick asks. "It's a common office supplies item that resembles the Jaws of Life."

"Where's the fun in that, O'G?"

"Flats are so tiresome."

Epiphany Noctchaw laughs.

"Poor Baby O'Grady got a pinch flat already," Rodd says. He takes off his helmet and sets it on a metal file cabinet covered with stickers. "Call Mitsuboshi Roadside Assistance next time."

Mick looks at Epiphany Noctchaw. She's expressionless. Mick jousts a knight off a buzzard. He runs his ostrich over the egg and collects 3,000 Survival Points.

Epiphany Noctchaw blows a bubble. She pops it with nice teeth. Asks Mick how long he's here for.

"Wednesday," Rodd responds for him. "He thinks."

"Entering the street contest seemed like a good idea," Mick says. "Back in July when I filled out the form and mailed it to 2-Hip 'in care of' Moon Babes Retire Bikes."

"You'll be alright," Rodd says. "NMM will have a tent at the event. New Mexico Medics. Your new friends Glorieta and Angelo."

"He filled out a form and mailed it?" Epiphany Noctchaw asks. "You mean like actually mailed it?"

"USPS," Rodd says. "Yes."

"Wow."

"Roots, toots."

"Bicycle City Express," Mick says.

"Grown men not using the Internet," Epiphany Noctchaw says. "I like it."

"Don't get us wrong," Rodd says. "We're against wasteful culture."

Impossible situation, Mick thinks. How can this get any worse? Six enemy knights. Lava troll. Now a pterodactyl. Oh, no. His last guy dies. Game over. Rodd laughs. He pats Mick on the shoulder and says he'll be right back with the Hooligan. It's hangin' in cold storage down in the basement.

"Underground," Mick says. "We'll be here."

"I'm moseyin'," Epiphany Noctchaw says. "Ciao."

She pulls back on the handlebars. Rollback. Rollout. Rad.

Rodd stops. He turns around. He says he thought she was supposed to work today?

"I am. Elina opened for me this mornin' so I could go pick up that outer space permit."

"Nice work, Noctchaw. Where is it?"

"Chat has it up front. I have another pallet to bring in from the dock then I am moseyin'."

"See you later."

"Ciao."

Mick watches her ride the forklift bike through the warehouse doors. Sign over the doors says:

SHOP

"Axle extenders," Rodd says.

"Huh?"

"I have to come up with two sets of pegs for the bikecar."

"Does the Hooligan have pegs?"

"All four."

"Radical, Moon."

"Be right back with it."

"You wouldn't happen to have a spare pouch of Big League Chew, would you?"

"Fresh out," Rodd says. "Wait'll you see this bikepark we're about to hit."

Chapter Fifteen

Ukai is 15. She runs a 14-tooth freewheel. Mick has a porcelain crown on *his* 14-tooth. Rodd laughs. Mick has no clue how much of a chore it is to find corresponding 39-tooth chainrings, Rodd says. He needs to score some more soon. Kid digs sprocket crunches and disasters.

How Ukai Moon rides Swirling Zagnut Bikepark reminds Mick how magical age 15 is.

She's got gold Ukai rims on Rodd's black Kuwahara KZ-1 from '82. Haro number plate. No brakes. Kashimax seat slammed all the way down on a layback post. Yellow Cycle Pro Snake Belly tires. Red 10-inch rise handlebars. Oakley II grips. Ukai carves a nose wheelie over a T-shaped door in a brick-banked wall. Laughs out loud as she lands.

"U!" Rodd calls out. "Yeah!"

Traces her line over the door. Now Mick has to do it. R.C. Alderman never did this. Neither did J.G. Garonzik.

Weightless.

He makes it.

Sketchy.

Swerves around a caravan of schoolchildren. They're probably playing the same game they are. Follow the Leader.

Cicadas buzz in the trees.

New Mexico locust.

MOON BABES OF BICYCLE CITY

Focus.
Ukai's freewheel clicks as she hovers over a six-foot-high volcano spray painted:

```
M   V   P
O   E   R
T   H   O
O   I   H
R   C   I
    L   B
    E   I
    S   T
        E
        D
```

Concrete poetry, Mick thinks.
He can't imagine who would ride a motor vehicle here.
He takes that back. He saw *Mad Max*. And *Werewolves on Wheels*.
Rodd blasts a one-handed Leary. Dayum! Mick didn't know Rodderick had that in his bag of tricks. His arsenal.
Mick hits the volcano and carves a "Crews." John Crews made up the jump. Crews was inducted to the BMX Hall of Fame in '06. Creator of bicycle motocross racing tool sets called Pit-Kits. Crews owned two bike shops in Northern California. Folsom, where the prison is.
So this is Swirling Zagnut Bikepark of B.C.
Considerable activity for high noon.
Mick craves a "Pineapple Sanford" thirst quencher that he saw advertised in a brochure at the airport. Third-part pineapple juice, third-part Super Socko sports drink, third-part Mello Yello served "on the rocks" in a Nora Cup.
Handrail train conducted by a kid in a tie-dye tank top. He icepicks the rail. Nice.
Next dude 50/50s it to barspin.

Man on an SE Fat Ripper tire-rides down the rail. Wildman.

Last kid grinds it to 180.

"Raliens!" Mick impersonates Scooby-Doo from *Scooby-Doo and the Alien Invaders*. No one hears him. "Reah!"

Freerider guy calls out, "Ramp to ramp!" Full-face helmet, flannel shirt, jeans, knee pads.

Ramp to ramp? Oh, Mick notices. Over the campers. Row of RVs.

Ukai follows him. Rodd follows her. Mick follows them.

Mick read something somewhere about this guy or he saw him on a video. Generation-removed grunge dude who rides an Airborne Toxin. Tuck no-hander over the RVs. Lands on the roof of the last one.

"Oh!"

Long-dive crash.

Dust cloud.

Dude gets up. Gets back on. Goes on. Tries to go on.

Chain is derailed.

Mick pedals up to Rodd and Ukai.

"David Munch," Rodd says. "Everyone calls him Muncher. 'Sloshy Muncher' is his showman name."

"Shaman?" Mick asks.

"Showman."

"Those recreational vehicles he just jumped," Mick says. "Don't tell me they're—"

"*Breaking Bad* RV Bikes," Rodd says. "Yeah, they sure are. Fleetwood Bounders. Identical replicas of the RV from the show."

"Isn't that illegal?"

"I told him he better call Saul."

"Told who?"

"I told his uncle Lawrence that," Rodd says. "Larry Munch. They sell hot grub, beverages, and other sundry products from 'em."

"Drugs?"

"No drugs. Candy and snacks. All the essential bike parts anyone'd ever need in a pinch. Larry lives in the RV at the beginning of the row."

"I'm goin' up to the pool, Dad," Ukai says.

"Which one?"

"Eagle Claw pool."

"Alright U. Don't forget now, there's no lifeguard on duty up there."

Ukai departs.

"Feast your eyes on the Krystal Ships of Psychotic Larry, O'Grady."

Chapter Sixteen

The door of the Krystal Ship at the beginning of the row opens. That's what Jesse Pinkman called his and Heisenberg's meth lab on *Breaking Bad*. Their battered RV up in Albuquerque. Beige with the brown, goldenrod, and rust stripes. It's one of a baker's dozen—13, Mick counts again—Krystal Ships that Sloshy Muncher says he needs to kick back in pronto.

Smoke trickles from the RV as its occupants emerge. They're wearing respirators and aprons. Mechanics, it appears. Detailers.

"A hundred percent recycled bicycles and found metal," Rodd says. "Now you know why we call him Psychotic Larry. It's rooted in reality."

"Five bullet holes in the doors?" Mick asks.

"Yes sir. Five per door. *Back* door is more accurate. Other side has a four-foot concession window. They're spaced out like this between the ramps because of the awnings."

Sloshy Muncher yawns. He takes off his helmet, unbuttons his flannel, headbangs his mane. He climbs into the first Bounder.

The Krystal Ship.

Rodd lays his bike down on the desert. He holds the door open for Mick. Mick shakes his head, No.

"No thanks. I'll stay out here. Out here on the perimeter."

"Ride around to the other side then."

Mick rides around the Bounder. The handle of a hydraulic floor jack has a Vans waffle grip on it. Mick bunnyhops it. So it's non-operational at the moment, this Krystal Ship that Sloshy Muncher says he needs to eat Chile Limón Funyuns in and finish his Flintstones soda. He raises his can of Cactus Cooler. "Cheers Betty," he says. He presses "EJECT" on a boom box, removes a cassette and flips it, reinserts it, shuts the door.

Presses the "PLAY" button.

Drums. Bass. Guitars. Grunge.

"Blood Circus," Mick says.

"You got it!" Sloshy Muncher says. He's shirtless. Conglomeration of necklaces. Must make some noise. No tattoos.

"How did you get that?" Rodd asks Mick.

"Their *Primal Rock Therapy* EP. I had it on CD. It included five extra tracks, I believe. Sub Pop Records, 1992."

"The year I was born," Sloshy Muncher says. He extends his hand through the window. "Hi, I'm Dave Munch."

Handshake.

"Mick O'Grady."

Two thousand nineteen minus nineteen ninety-two. Mick does the math. Dave Munch is 27.

"Tell O'Grady what he wins," Rodd says.

Dave is looking into the video camera mounted on top of his helmet. He polishes the lens with his flannel. He holds the helmet at an angle. Sets it down on a countertop inside the Bounder.

"What happened, Cap'n Crunch?"

"Forgot I was wearin' these pads, that's what happened," Dave says. "Or else I wouldn't have gone for that tuck." He removes a knee pad. "They got stuck under my bars. I was practicin' front-flip jumps up on Fidge Ridge and I landed every one I tried, too. Long-distance front flips."

"*With* the bike," Rodd says.

"With the bike, right." He winces. "Ah, shooting pain. Side stitch. I'll be alright."

"Reminded me of Evel Knievel at Caesar's Palace," Rodd says. "Viva Knievel."

"I saw that movie *Viva Knievel*!" Dave says. "That guy from *The Naked Gun* was in it. White-haired dude wearin' a three-piece suit. He was the drug smuggler. What's his name?"

"Leslie Nielsen?" Mick asks.

"Yeah! Him. My uncle has it on video tape somewhere around here. My great uncle, I should say."

"Great uncle to have," Mick says.

"He's my grandfather's brother."

"He's a PBE legend, is what he is," Rodd says. "Punk Bike Enduro legend. Larry was a force to be reckoned with." Rodd chews a Funyun. "NorCal Fat Tire Flyer. Seventy-five."

"He's 75?" Mick asks.

"Nineteen seventy-five. Larry and his brother Warren were two o' the craziest competitors in NorCal. So loco they named their team Marin County Organ Donors. Factory MCOD. Imagine racin' with your coaster brake locked up down the most gnarliest mountain trails ever! Locked up outta necessity because it was so burly."

"Sadistic descents," Mick says. "I've had my share of those."

"Totally demented," Rodd goes on. "Blazin' full speed with no front brakes or suspension. Goin' for the fastest time recorded on a nuclear green stopwatch they had. The stopwatch had a Beck's beer bottle cap coverin' the reset switch. I think Larry came up with that little modification. How old is he now, Muncher?"

"He just turned 68."

"So he was like 25 at the time. Wasn't he?"

"Yeah."

"Larry's brother Warren was two years older. Warren passed away in '93. Rest in Peace, War."

"I'm sorry to hear that, Dave," Mick says.

"Ah, thanks man. I was one year old."

"Muncher's dad Al and his mom Olive and his great uncle Larry moved the family out here after that." Rodd opens a can of Cactus Cooler. "'Down and out here' as our saying goes. After War passed in Sacramento. Cheers Betty."

Down and Out Here, Mick thinks. Down and Out Here in Bicycle City, New Mexico.

"The 'Limón' is strong in these ones," Rodd says. "Whew, are they hot. Spicy."

"See this?" Dave asks Mick.

"What?"

"See this guitar pick?"

Mick rolls closer to the concession window. The necklace pendant is a guitar pick. "EV" over white stars on a blue "V" outlined in red.

"I knew Evel Knievel was a painter but I didn't know he played guitar," Mick says.

Dave laughs.

"Evel didn't play. It's an Eddie Vedder guitar pick from 2009. Eddie threw it out to the crowd at a Pearl Jam show and my mom picked it up in the pit. My dad said as soon as he saw what was on it, he felt like I should have it. Because *his* dad Warren was such a big fan of Evel Knievel."

Rodd asks Mick if he can guess who made it into a necklace.

Mick nods.

He doesn't need to say it.

Decides to say it anyway.

"Psychotic Larry."

CLUB HOME BOY

psychotic Larry

Chapter Seventeen

"You're goddam right," Rodderick Moon says.

Chapter Eighteen

Moon, you lunatic. Imitating Walter White from *Breaking Bad* back there. Heisenberg.
  Rodd laughs. "Convincing impression?"
  "I was already convinced," Mick says. "Wholly."
  "So what is your story, O'Grady? Sorry I cut you off."
  "Tryin' to crash me?"
  "Yes, I was. So what's happenin'?"
  "Like I said before," Mick says. "I've been tryin' to figure that out. As we go along, I guess."
  "Freestylin'?"
  "Pretty much. Yes."
  "What did you think of Elina's?"
  "We just breezed by, bruh," Mick says.
  "What is this? Tongue twisters?"
  Mick laughs. He could see that as an ad.

    We just breezed by, bruh.
    Elina's.

"Bummed that it's a Trick Bar, not a Strip Bar?"
"Elated," Mick says. "I knew that though. Silly."
"How? We're not online."
"I read about it in a PDF."

"Message board in a massage parlor?"

"Formatted PDF on a USB. Bootleg."

"I hope you're kidding," Rodd says. "You know how I feel about that. E.T.—Elina's Thrusters—is set up like the 'Bicycle Boogie' scene in *RAD: The Movie* was. Themed riding rooms."

"I didn't see that part," Mick says.

"Huh? How could you have missed that?"

"In the afore-mentioned PDF, I meant."

"Oh, I was gonna say," Rodd says. "I thought you meant in *RAD*. Ms. Melvina can't wait to meet you, by the way."

Mick and Rodd approach the hull of a space probe.

Mick recalls reading about these relics in a brochure at Cavern City Air Terminal in Carlsbad, New Mexico. "Roadside Attractions You Can Get Rad In!" the brochure had said. Feels like days ago.

This morning, 'twas.

"Archaic," Rodd says. He stands up on the pedals of his GJS. "Here's the hull of a probe from the Viking Surveyor program, '66 to '72. Hit it."

Rodd cranks.

Mick follows him.

Rodd carves the interior of the hull.

Hull. Holy hull.

Graffiti-rich so it's slippery.

Mick makes it.

Rodd is seated now. Coasting. No-handed.

"Once capable of 100,000 feet," he says. "Self-propelled sonic flight."

"Massive," Mick says. "Air."

"Three hundred forty-three thousand feet is the edge of space," Rodd says.

"Word?"

"Did you see that Patterson by the dirt jumps?" Rodd asks.

"It was a Parkinson," Mick says.

"Zounds. I'm surprised you noticed that."
"Old school BMX logo rip. Low seat tipped me off that it wasn't a Patterson. Oversized tubing. Brakelessness. I never heard of Parkinson."
"U.K."
Mick nods.
"Yo," Mick says. "I'm gonna need a nap when we get to your pad. Few and sundry snacks from my backpack and a nap. This is getting ridiculous."
"Understandable, Old Sport. Dinner is at 6:43."
"The half-baggie of Blue Sky rock candy I had back at the RV is about all that's keepin' me goin'."
"Go on, goon."
"Blueberry."
"Rogue prototype BikeCardoba alert," Rodd says. "Here they come apedalin' it. Hell-cats at the helm. Wild and wooly."

Mick's already been hearing it. Liking it.

Animated banter between babes. Amplified over the PA system. Laughter now out the speakers.

Sounds like Mudhoney in the background.

Something off *Superfuzz Bigmuff* (1988). Yeah, "Mudride."

Close enough to see cleavage.

They're careening.

Russ Meyer Lives. Here.

Rolling tumbleweed. The BikeCardoba disintegrates it. Roostertail of desert dirt and debris.

"Careful everybody," Rodd says. "Rocks!"

BikeCardoba stops. Passenger rider Babe—Moon Babe?—tosses a handful of stickers out the window.

Occupants emerge, laughing. Flat-ironed jet-black bob cut driver and big hair—massive hair, Mick muses—passenger rider.

Looks like a zine the latter has.

She hands it to Mick.

Perfumed.

"Every time one of these stops there's an old school jam, isn't there?" Mick asks.

"Jam alright," Massive Hair says. "Get in."

Cheek hollowing drag. Exhale. In Mick's face.

Flat-Iron Jet-Black has a cordless reporter-style microphone in hand. It has MTV logos and a black lightning bolt on it. The mic, not her hand. Chrome fingernail polish.

"Abduction?" Rodd asks. "Alien abduction? Interesting development, O'Grady. Well I guess you can take a nap on the hammock in their basement. See you at Fennelseed's snake run bonfire. Later."

Chapter Nineteen

Mick turns on the Trunk Interior Light with some difficulty.
　He reads "Chapter XX":

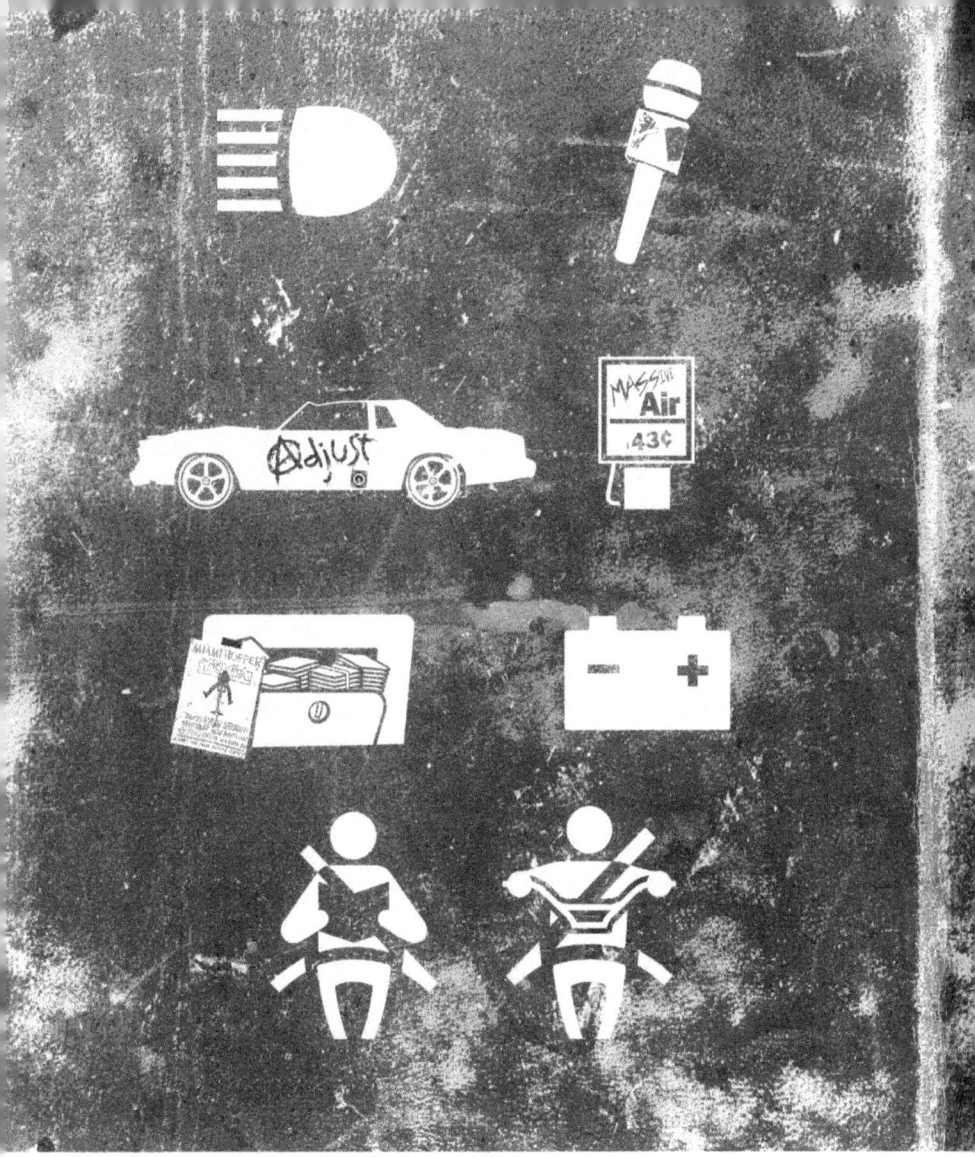

MOON MAN & THEM'S

2020 BIKECARDOBA
Operating Instructions and Product Information

Introducing

You have chosen to ride a Moon Man and Them's 2020 BikeCardoba, a product in which design and construction have received the care that quality demands.

You may have previously ridden a Moon Man and Them's product or perhaps this is your first. In either case—for your own benefit and that of your passenger(s)—please read through this owner's manual before you lose it. It won't be online and it won't be reprinted. Repopping is forbidden. Even though you may have been riding for years, certain features of this BikeCardoba may be new to you and in the pages that follow, you will find information that will be helpful.

You may have heard about the bikecar packed with C-4 that exploded outside Tabletop Tavern in 2011. No one was injured in the blast. We had nothing to do with that.

We wish you safe and pleasant riding.

Rodderick Moon
Moon Man & Them's
Moon Babes Retire Bikes

Moon Man & Them's reserves the right to make changes in design and specs, and/or to make additions to or improvements in its products without imposing any obligations upon itself to install them on products previously manufactured and/or womanufactured.

Off to a Good Start

A Word About Your Keys
Lose 'em? We got you.

A small numbered metal tag is attached to each set of keys. The number on this tag can be used to either duplicate keys from your dealer or from a locksmith. After recording the number, you should retain the tag in a safe place. If you did not receive tags with your keys, ask your dealer to give you the number.

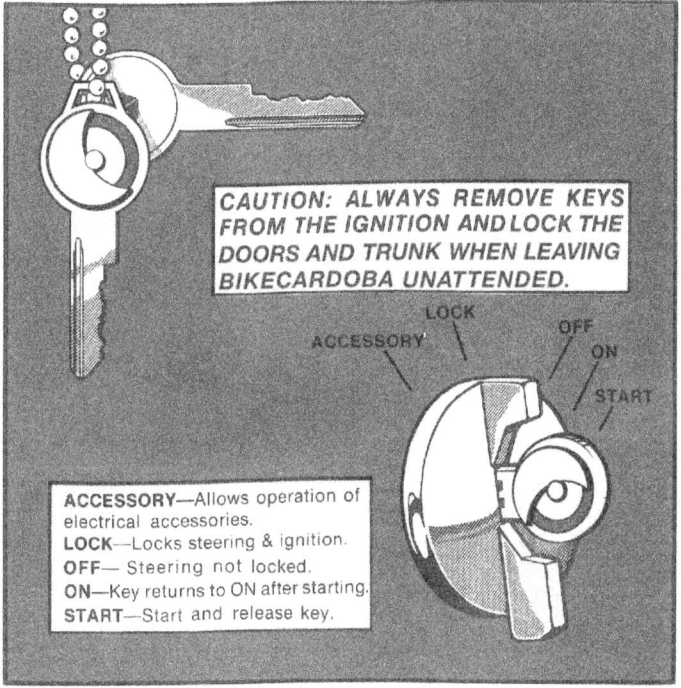

CAUTION: ALWAYS REMOVE KEYS FROM THE IGNITION AND LOCK THE DOORS AND TRUNK WHEN LEAVING BIKECARDOBA UNATTENDED.

ACCESSORY—Allows operation of electrical accessories.
LOCK—Locks steering & ignition.
OFF— Steering not locked.
ON—Key returns to ON after starting.
START—Start and release key.

Key Reminder Buzzer
If the driver's door is opened when the key is in the ignition lock, a buzzer will sound to remind you to remove the key.

Ignition Sequence Start & Steering Lock

The key can be inserted or withdrawn only in the "Lock" position.

Ignition Switch Lamp

The switch is lighted when the driver rider's door is opened. The lamp will remain on for approximately 43 seconds after the door is closed to facilitate inserting the key.

> **Note:** 2020 BikeCardoba has a column mounted gear selector. The key cannot be turned to "Lock" until the selector is in the "Park" position.
>
> Do not attempt to pull the shift lever out of "Park" or "Rollback" after the key is in the "Lock" position.

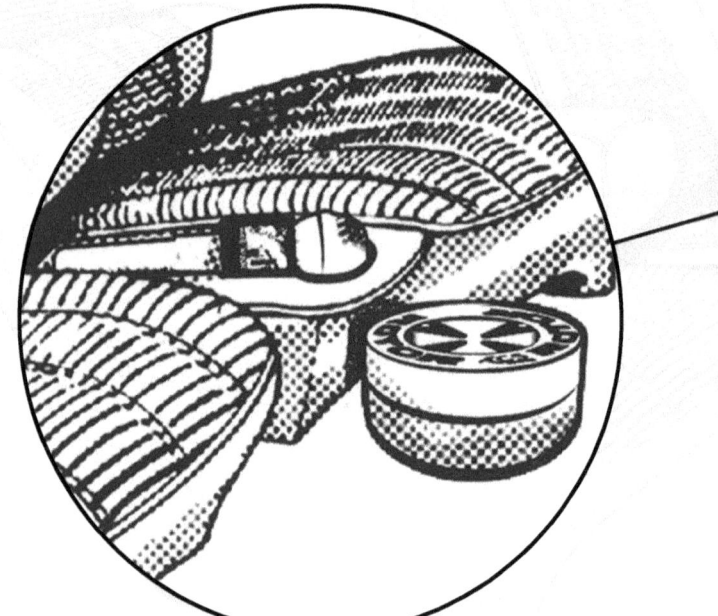

Bucket Seats – Mirrors

Seat Adjustment

The adjusting lever is located at the door side of the driver rider's seat. The front bucket seats also have an adjusting lever on the passenger rider's door side of the seat.

Reclining Front Seats /
Cordless Reporter-Style Microphone (in Console) /
ACS Rotor Beverage Holder

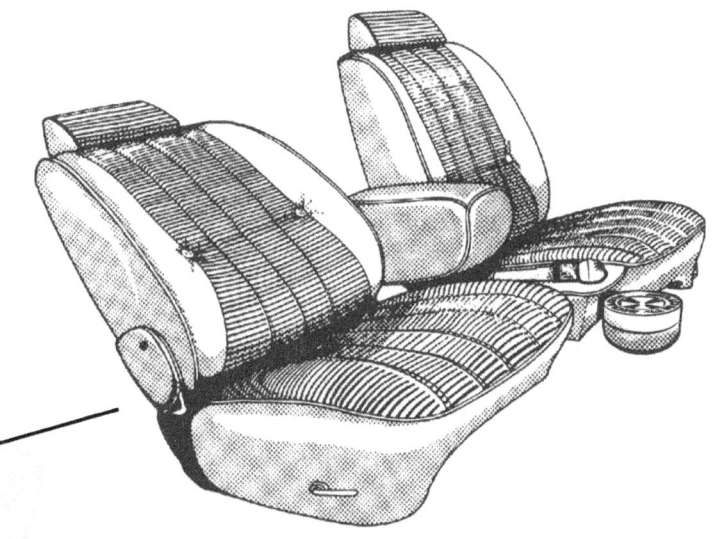

Power Seat Adjustment

The power seat adjuster provides six-way adjustment of the front bucket seats. The center switch moves the seat up or down and forward or backward.

Instrument and Controls

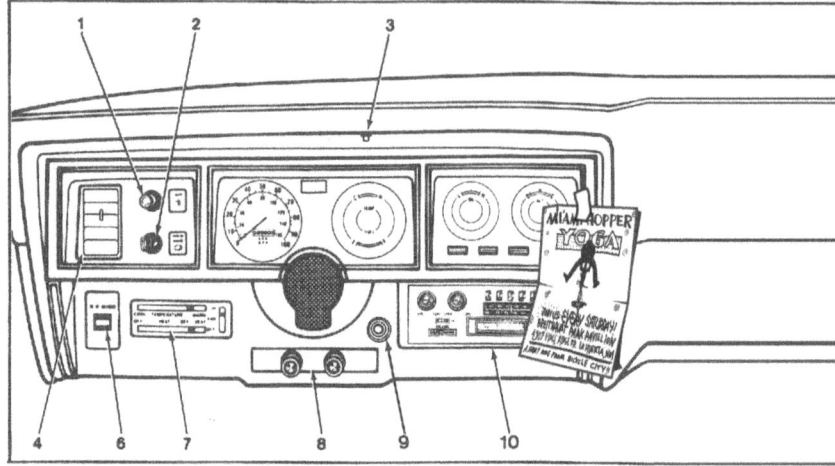

1 Headlight Switch
2 Wiper/Washer Control
3 Map Light
4 Air Conditioner Outlets
4A Upper Level
   Ventilation Outlets
5 Digital Clock
6 Accessory Switches

Full-Tilt Bozo
The front switch tilts the front of the seat and the rear switch tilts the rear of the seat. *Adjust*

Head Restraints
Padded head restraints for the front bucket seats reduce the risk of whiplash injury in the event of an impact from the rear. Head restraints are adjustable vertically. The upper edge should be set as high as possible, at least at the level of the ears.

Seatback Release
For access to the rear seat, it is necessary to release the front seat locking mechanism. The release is conveniently located on the rear outside edge of the seatback. David Lee Roth Mod Kit is available if you want to reach down between your legs and ease the seat back. Made in Panama.

– 2020 BikeCardoba

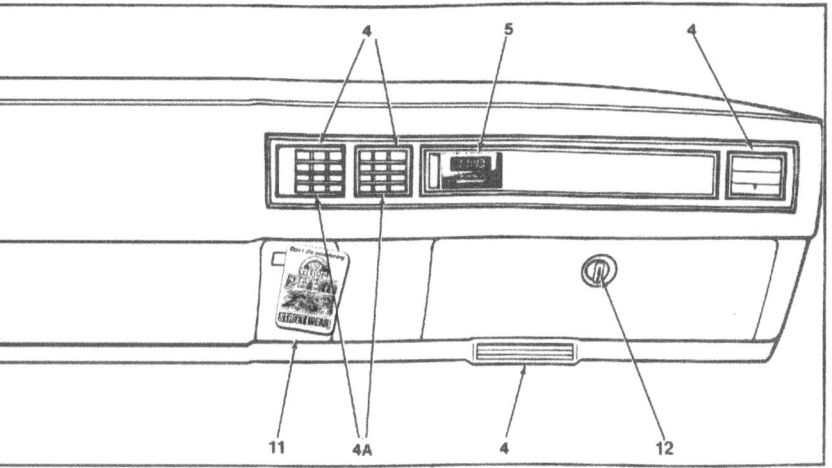

7 Heater or A/C Controls
8 Fresh Air Vent Control
9 Remote Control Mirror (Right Side)
10 Radio (Concuss)
11 Ash Tray and Lighter
12 Glove Box Lock and Release

Rear View Mirror (*Vs.*,[2] 1993)
The rear view mirror should be adjusted to center on the view through the rear window. Bothersome headlight glare can be reduced by moving the small control under the mirror to the nighttime position.

Side View Mirrors
To receive maximum benefit, adjust the outside mirrors to center on the adjacent lane of traffic with a slight overlap of the view obtained on the inside mirror. Knock them off with a two-by-four if there's a ceremony that's about to begin. Same with the handles on the doors.

---

[2] Pearl Jam's second album.

MASTER CLUSTER DETAILS – BIKECARDOBA

Master Cluster Details

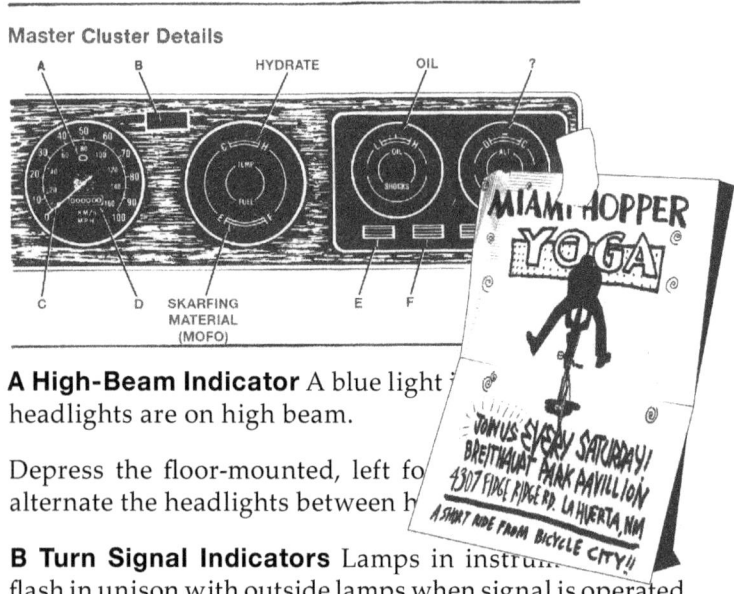

A High-Beam Indicator A blue light indicates headlights are on high beam.

Depress the floor-mounted, left foot switch to alternate the headlights between high and low.

B Turn Signal Indicators Lamps in instrument flash in unison with outside lamps when signal is operated.

C Speedometer Indicated speed in Miles Per Hour and Kilometers Per Hour for overseas operation.

D Odometer Indicates total distance the BikeCardoba has been ridden.

E Seat Belt Reminder Light and Buzzer The "FASTEN SEAT BELTS" lamp will be illuminated for 43 seconds when the ignition switch is turned to the "ON" position. If the rider has not fastened the seat belt a buzzer will also sound during the same interval.

F Brake System Warning Lamp The warning lamp will light when the brake lever is depressed if a failure has occurred in either half of the dual braking system—rear and/or front. If the light comes on, the cause should be determined and corrected as soon as possible. Continued operation of the BikeCardoba is dangerous, unless you know what you're doing riding brakeless. After the condition is corrected, a heavy application of the brake is necessary to turn the light off.

Operation

Parking Brake (Locking Levers)
When the ignition switch is in the "ON" position, the red "BRAKE" light in the instrument master cluster indicates when the parking brake is applied. When stopped, place the gear selector in the "Park" position. *Moon Babes of Bicycle City* Bike Club Member #005 "Custom Mike" Sarris uses front brake locking levers. He locks his front brake to do The Miami Stopper. Most of us only ever used rear brake locking levers. Set the parking brakes firmly by pulling both brake levers and pressing the locking buttons.

Ash Tray and Lighter
An ashtray and lighter are located at the right of the instrument panel. Only girls can smoke in here.

Column Mounted Selector
The selector lever is mounted on the right side of the steering column. To ride, move the selector lever from "Park" or "Neutral" to the desired ride position.

GEAR RANGES

"P" Park
BikeCardoba's ignition turns on and off in this range.

"RB" Rollback
Shift into this range only after the BikeCardoba has come to a complete stop, or upon achieving semblance of 180.

"N" Neutrals
Range used for towing and pushing purposes.

"H'B" Haulin' Bazoonies
For long-distance high speed cruise control. Also for descending steep grades such as mountain trails.

"R" Ride
Primary gear for most bike path and street riding. Ride. Just ride.

"G" Granny
For riding uphill.

Shifting Gears
Shift through each gear in order. Upshift from G to R to H'B. Downshift from H'B to R to G.

LIGHTS

Headlights and Parking Lights
The headlights and parking lights are turned on by the "two position" headlight switch. Rotating the same switch regulates panel lighting brightness.

Headlights & Parking Lights

 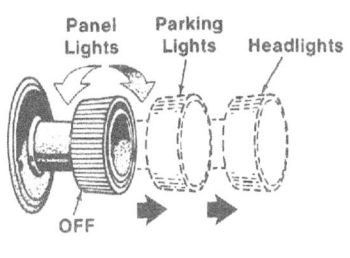

Lights-On Reminder
If the headlights or parking lights are left on inadvertently after the ignition is turned off, a buzzer will sound when either door is opened. 43 seconds.

Interior Lights
All courtesy, reading, pillar, map, and dome lamps are turned on by opening a door, turning the headlight switch fully left, or by a switch on the lamp fixture.

Hazard Warning Flasher
The flasher switch is located on the steering column just under the GT stem holding the Peregrine handlebars and ODI Mushroom II grips. Pull out the flasher switch and all front and rear directional signals will intermittently flash.

This is an emergency warning system. It is not intended for when the BikeCardoba is in motion. If it is necessary to leave the vehicle to go for service, the Hazard Warning Flasher system will continue to operate even with the ignition key removed.

Turn Signal with Bike Lane Change Feature
For changing lanes or when making a gradual turn, the lever may be held in the "bike lane change" position. It will return to a neutral position when released.

The fully engaged position is for use when making a normal turn or when roosting for bonus points. The signal will remain on until the normal turn is completed or until the lever is returned to neutral by hand.

Lamps in the instrument master cluster and on top of the front fenders flash to indicate proper operation of the front and rear turn signal lamps. If the indicator lamp remains on and does not flash, check for a defective outside lamp bulb. If the indicator lamp fails to light when the lever is moved it would suggest that the fuse or indicator bulb has burned out.

Door Locks
Each door will lock if the lock plunger is down when the door is closed. Therefore, be sure the keys are not inside the BikeCardoba.

Two separate operations are required to open the doors from the inside (except driver rider's side door) once they are locked. First, the lock plunger must be raised and then the door handle can be pulled. The driver's door may be opened without first raising the plunger.

Horn
There is a possibility that the contact point that actuates your horn is not in the same location as on your car, truck, van, or whatever vehicle you drive. Friendly Reminder: Motor Vehicles Prohibited in Bicycle City, New Mexico. Take a minute to be sure that you will automatically depress the correct pressure point if the need to alert others occurs.

Windshield Wipers

To operate the windshield wiper, push lever right to select desired speed. Fully left is "Off" position. Fully.

Windshield Wiper/Washer

Windshield Washers

Newspaper and glass cleaner works best on the Plexiglas® windshield and windows. Bonus points in reference to Cru Jones delivering *USA T* on his newspaper route in *RAD: The Movie.*

When seated inside the BikeCardoba, press down on the wiper control to operate the washer. Pressing down the wiper control also operates the windshield wipers at low speed. To stop the wipers, move the wiper control to the "Off" position.

Accessories

RADIO (CONCUSS)
All Moon Man & Them's radios are described in the "Sound System" manual included in your Operator's Manual literature package.

REPORTER-STYLE MICROPHONE
Mic check.

PA SYSTEM
Check.

LOUDSPEAKER
Check.

Air Conditioner Controls

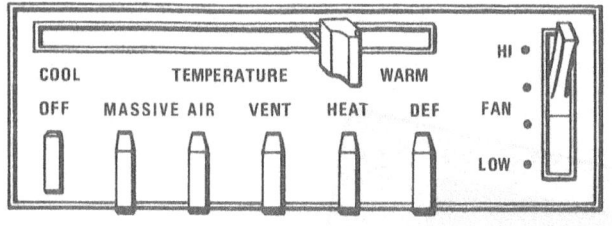

AIR CONDITIONER
This factory installed unit combines air conditioning, ventilation, heating, and defrosting into one efficient year-round system. See **Frank Garrido**.

Vacuum Fluorescent Electronic Swatchometer Digital Clock

A vacuum fluorescent digital read-out indicates the time in hours and minutes when the ignition switch is in the "ON" position. To set the correct time, advance the hour or minute setting by pressing the rocker switch located below the display window.

Remote Trunk Lid Release

The trunk lid can be unlocked and opened from inside the BikeCardoba by pressing a switch located in the glove compartment. Release will operate only with the ignition switch in the "ON" position.

When the ignition key must be left with the BikeCardoba, such as for service or parking lot attendants, be sure that the glove box is locked to prevent unauthorized access to the trunk compartment.

Power Door Locks

Both doors can be locked and unlocked from the inside by a switch on the strange days door arm rest.

Electrically Operated Sunroof

The sunroof is operated by a two-position control switch located on the forward center area of the roof header.

If necessary, the roof can be closed manually by using the Blue-Sky crank handle provided in the glove compartment. Redline Flight Crank Arm handle available at participating dealers.

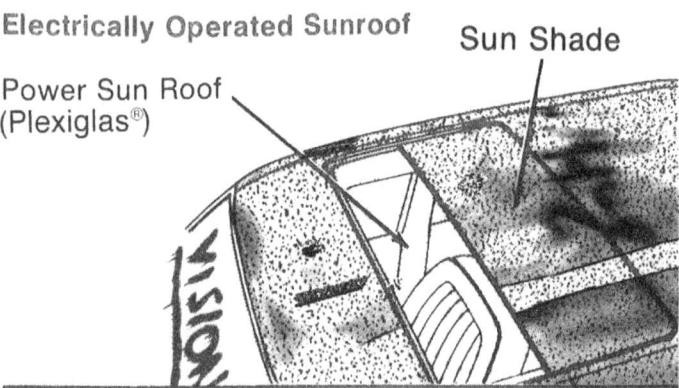

Electrically Operated Sunroof   Sun Shade
Power Sun Roof (Plexiglas®)

If equipped with a tinted Plexiglas® sun roof, care should be taken in cleaning the inside surface of the sunroof window. Use non-abrasive cleaners only and a soft parade cloth.

> **Maintenance** – Periodically clean and lubricate the guide rails. Remove the plug and tighten the screw.

Peregrine Q Handlebars

To tilt the steering assembly, simply lift the small lever below the turn signal control and move the Peregrine Q handlebars up or down as desired then release the lever to lock the bars firmly in place.

Tilt Steering Wheel

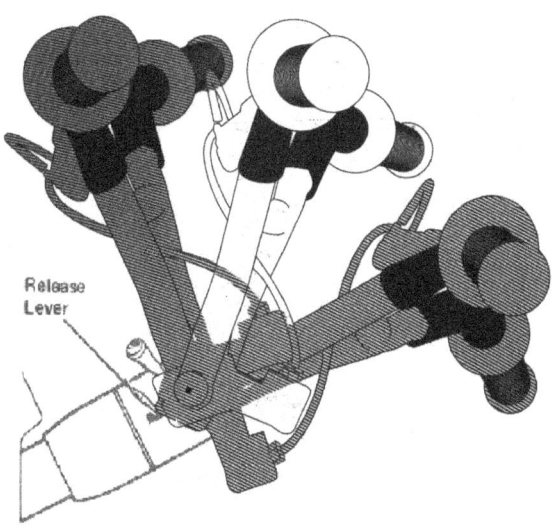

Tires and Vehicle Loading

Proper tire inflation pressure is essential to the safe and satisfactory operation of your vehicle. Three primary areas are affected by improper tire pressure:

1 Safety – Under-inflation increases tire flexing and can result in tire/tube failure. Over-inflation results in a tire losing its ability to cushion shock. Objects on the road and pot holes could cause tire injury that may result in tire failure.

2 Economy – Improper inflation pressures cause uneven wear patterns to develop across the tire tread. The abnormal wear patterns will radically reduce tread life resulting in a need for earlier tire replacement. Under-inflation also increases tire rolling resistance and can cause ultra hardcore cardio, yo.

3 Ride Comfort and Vehicle Stability – Proper tire inflation contributes to a comfortable ride. Over-inflation produces a jarring and uncomfortable ride but some riders like that. Both under-inflation and over-inflation affect the stability characteristics of the BikeCardoba and can produce a feeling of sluggish response or over-responsiveness. Unequal tire pressures can cause erratic and unpredictable steering response.

Tire Inflation Pressures
The proper tire pressure for your BikeCardoba is listed on a placard attached to the left front door lifter puller. The pressure should be checked and adjusted before each weekly church meeting. Check more often if BikeCardoba is subject to a wide range of outdoor temperatures as tire pressures vary with temperature changes. Daily.

Inflation pressures specified on the placard are always "cold inflation pressure." Cold inflation pressure is defined as the tire pressure after the vehicle has not been ridden for at least three hours, or driven less than a mile after a three hour period. The cold inflation pressure must not exceed the maximum values molded onto the tire sidewall.

Tire pressures may increase from 2 to 6 psi during operation. Do NOT reduce this normal pressure build-up.

Tire Size and Types
Only tires shown in the "Allowable Tire and Wheel Size" chart may be used on your vehicle. Do not install tires smaller than the minimum size shown on the tire inflation placard located on the vehicle.

Oversize tires do not provide increased vehicle capacity. They do however provide an extra margin of tread life.

The speedometer of your vehicle is geared for the original equipment tires. If tires different in size from originally installed are used, ask your dealer if a change of the speedometer drive pinion is necessary to give a correct reading. Keep reading.

Trailer Towing
The trailer hitch weight and tongue load must be considered as part of the maximum vehicle capacity when loading the BikeCardoba.

For trailer towing, inflate the rear tires to 88 psi.

Jacking and Tire Changing
The jack supplied with the BikeCardoba should only be used for fixing flats, changing wheels and tires, or for placing factory-approved jackstands under the chassis. Never work under the vehicle while the jack is being used as the only means of support.

Rad Padded gurneys and notched jackstands are available for those who want to do bench press exercises using the BikeCardoba.

> **Note:** Two spotters minimum are advised for safety purposes during weight training-related activities. Don't listen to Nitzer Ebb. Shit's garbage. Shirley Manson though, sure. Garbage, you know? Nineties radio. Love songs even. Any era.

Follow the instructions carefully to reduce the risk of the BikeCardoba falling off the jack.

First park the BikeCardoba on a hard level surface. Jack only on level ground. Flat land.

Engage the locking lever for the opposite wheels.

Warning: Do not attempt to change a tire or wheel on the side of the BikeCardoba close to moving traffic. Pull far enough off the street to avoid the danger of being hit when operating the jack or changing the wheel.

- Activate the Hazard Warning Flasher.

- Block the front and rear of the wheel diagonally oppositethe jacking position. Use the supplied two-by-four sections with Snakebelly tire treads nailed underneath them for this purpose.

- Passengers should not remain in the BikeCardoba when the BikeCardoba is jacked, including trunk occupant(s).

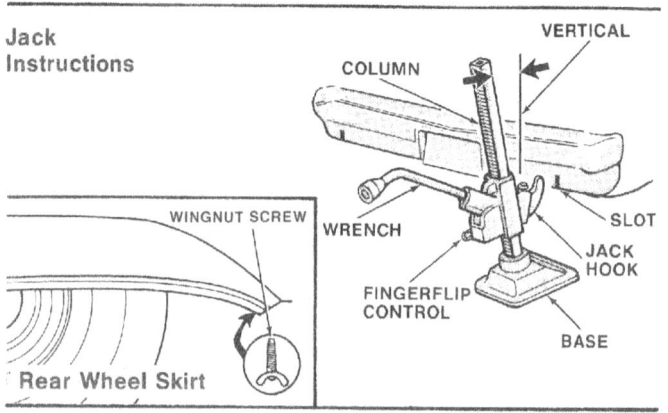

Tire Rotation
All tires should be rotated at least every 4,130 miles and should be in correct balance to obtain uniform tread wear. Tire inspection at every other church meeting is recommended. If irregular tread wear has developed, rotation is suggested. Consult your dealer to determine the cause of irregular tread wear. Be sure to adjust tire pressure after rotating.

Skyway Axle Extenders
When *did* axle pegs become "passenger foot rests"? Axle extenders, not pegs.

Appearance
Your dealer offers a complete line of products for cleaning vinyl tops, upholstery, shag carpeting, tire skinwalls, and for brightening metal. Follow the instructions on each product container.

Paint and Trim
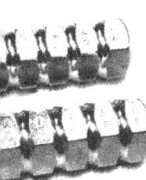
Your BikeCardoba is exposed to corrosive effects of salt spray, road film, and chemical fall out. Trick stars will want to hose it down often to protect not only the paint and trim but also the many exposed mountings and fixtures. Prompt washing may not thoroughly remove all of these deposits. Additional cleaners may be required.

If desired, use Moon Babes of Bicycle City Roark Polish on your BikeCardoba. Follow directions on container. Smiles, everyone. Smiles.

Damage to the Finish
Stone chips, fractures, or deep scratches in the finish should be promptly repaired unless your BikeCardoba is about to become a contest prop or obstacle. Exposed metal will quickly corrode and may develop into a condition requiring costly repairs.

Minor damage can be repaired by using touch-up materials available at your dealer. More extensive damage should be corrected in your dealer's body and paint facility. Otherwise, bashguard-bombs away brothers.

SANDING
Prior to repainting, sanding is recommended.

Using a 43-grit sanding disc, remove paint from the BikeCardoba body in minutes. Sand randomly in every direction you can think of to avoid grooves and other dings.

If pressed for time, at least scuff the stock shiny surface so the new layers of material will stick to it.

ACTION PAINTING (POLLAK)
People may have problems repainting their BikeCardobas. Real serious problems sometimes. Easy to forget that fact sometimes.

Exterior Body Trim
Complete paint jobs call for all exterior body trim to be removed. Using two-by-fours and other found objects in the contest area, knock off as much body trim as you can in the ceremony that's about to begin.

Waterproof Epoxy Primer
Waterproof epoxy primer provides primo corrosion resistance and exceptional adhesion capabilities for whatever particular exterior paint you've chosen. Make sure you use primer made for aluminum surfaces such as bikecar bodies made from recycled aluminum cans of Jolt Cola.

Protect Bare Metal
Mix the primer with a hardener according to instructions and apply with a spraygun. A second coat is recommended.

Some primers absorb water. If your BikeCardoba sports

only a primer finish, resist temptations to wash it in a wet t-shirt contest or ride it in the rain while wearing NOS JT Racing wet weather gloves.

If moisture finds its way into the primer, it can become trapped. Primer-surfacer is a porous, talc-based material similar to '80s goth makeup and moisture may remain there after the paint has been sprayed and cured.

Care of Skyway Tuff Wheels
Frequent cleaning is recommended to reduce the possibility of road film build-up or corrosion of conformity. Do not use steel wool to clean mag wheels. Soft Scrub.

Safety

Security Against Theft
Roughly 1.5 million bicycles are stolen each year. More than 180,000 are never recovered.

Always close the windows, remove the keys, and lock all doors when leaving the BikeCardoba unattended. Even if it's parked in your own driveway or garage. Try to park in a clean, well-lighted place. Thank you Ernest Hemingway.

If possible, park in a protected area. Never invite theft by leaving articles of value such as cassette tape collections exposed inside the BikeCardoba.

Safety Checks You Should Make Outside the BikeCardoba

Tires – Examine tires for excessive tread wear or uneven wear patterns. Check for stones, nails, staples, glass, or other objects lodged in the tread. Inspect for tread cuts or sidewall cracks. Check tires for proper pressure and mag wheel axle extenders for tightness.

Lights – Have someone observe the operation of all exterior lights while you activate the controls. Check turn signal and high beam indicator lights on the instrument panel.

Fluid leaks – Check area under BikeCardoba after overnight parking for water or other fluid leaks like Gatorade and coconut water and shit.

General Maintenance

Battery Care

Caution: Keep flame or sparks away from filler holes. Explosive hydrogen gas may be present.

Remove all caps and check water and electrolyte fluid level every two months (more often in hot weather or on long trips). The fluid should be at the bottom of the filler hole. Do not overfill. Check specific gravity once a year. Cable clamps should be tight on terminal posts and free of corrosion. Neutralize corrosion by washing with a solution of baking soda and water. Apply grease to the posts and clamps after tightening.

Windshield Wiper Blades

Periodic cleaning of the wiper blades is suggested to remove the accumulation of sand, bugs, salt, and road film. The wiper blades, arms, and windshield should be cleaned with a sponge, cloth, or a sheet of *USA Today* and glass cleaner. If the blades continue to streak or smear, they should be replaced.

> **Note:** Do not operate wipers for long periods on dry Plexiglas®; doing so accelerates deterioration of the rubber elements.

Front Suspension Ball Joints

All Moon Man & Them's BikeCardobas have two upper and two lower front suspension ball joints that require periodic servicing. These ball joints should be inspected twice a year, or whenever a BikeCardoba is serviced for other reasons. Damaged seals should be replaced to prevent leakage or contamination of the grease. Ball joints should also be replaced when the end play exceeds the spec outlined in the Front Suspension and Steering Linkage section of the Service Manual.

Steering Linkage
All Moon Man & Them's BikeCardobas have four Tie Rodd End Ball Joints and a Pinkman-type Arm Joint that require periodic servicing. These should be inspected twice a year, or whenever the BikeCardoba is serviced for other reasons. Damaged seals should be replaced to prevent leakage or contamination of the grease.

Upper and Lower Control Arm
Upper and lower control arm Brazilian bushings should be inspected for an off-center condition of inner metal in relation to outer metal. Total failure is evident by excessive movement within the bushings and noise caused by metal-to-metal contact. Small cracks in the outer rubber O-rings does not constitute failure.

Lower control arm bushings may be visually inspected by lifting the BikeCardoba on a hoist and inspecting by removing the front wheels. If failure has occurred, replace bushing(s) as recommended in the Service Manual.

Drivetrain Chains
Inspect chains for stretch and damage and replace if necessary. Check chains for proper tension and adjust if necessary, according to the specifications outlined in the Service Manual.

Rear Axles
When servicing the rear axle, always elevate both rear wheels. Do not rotate the axle by use of the Cook Bros. cranks or other means unless both wheels are elevated.

Buying Replacement Parts

Replacement parts are readily available from many bicycle sources, falling into one of four categories: Authorized Dealer Parts Departments, Local Bike Shops, Online Mail Order, and Black Market.

1. Authorized Dealer Parts Departments
Moon Babes Retire Bikes' warehouse in Bicycle City, New Mexico, is the primary source for parts that are unique to the BikeCardoba: struts, shocks, Miami Hopper Yoga flyers, trim pieces, and the like.

2. Local Bike Shops
Adobe. Brick and mortar. Decent shops stock frequently needed components that tend to wear out quickly such as tires, brake parts, chains, and grips. These shops often supply brand-new, new old stock (NOS), and/or reconditioned parts on an exchange basis, which can save considerable amounts of cash.

Discount auto parts stores are the best places to buy or order light bulbs, fuses, general accessories, paint, and touch-up paint. Hardware stores are handy for tools, pop beverages, and The Candy Machine.

3. Online Mail Order
You're on your own.

4. Black Market
See "3".

Stripping
Threads of a bolt, bolt hole, or nut can become stripped, usually from overtightening or using the wrong tools. Aluminum parts are very susceptible because aluminum is so soft that it is easily stripped.

Luckily, internal or external threads are often only partially stripped. After they've been cleaned up a bit with a tap or die, they will work. Plural for "die" is "dies". Sometimes you're simply fooked for Fook's sake. Bent over and banged.

If the latter applies, there's a slight chance you may still be able to drill and tap the hole to the next suitable oversize and install a larger diameter bolt, screw, or stud.

Trailer Towing
We recommend the BikeCardoba be towed from the front with the front wheels off the ground. Insert hitch of trailer into the "gasoline filler tube" behind the rear license plate. Trailers that weigh over 143 lbs. must be equipped with their own brakes.

Oh, the Sidepull Caliper Brakes (and Reverse-Sidepull Brakes on the Passenger Rider's Side)
Search YouTube. Follow the general maintenance and adjustment tips for caliper brakes or take it to a reputable dealer.

Printed In U.S.A.

Fictions are what we make of ourselves, and they cannot help reflecting something of our character and forecasting something of our fate.

    R. P. BLACKMUR, Introduction to *American Short Novels*[3] (1960)

Chapter XXI

Mick types an open letter on a Sears manual that Psychotic Larry has wired for sound. The tabletop it's on has a Potts Mod for the cord courtesy of Terrycable. Public Address system. Mick likes what he hears. He's phoneless, laptopsterless, they even confiscated his notebooks and pencils. Erasers. Moon Babes of Bicycle City erasers. His 2019 Colony BMX Oz-One has arrived from home and it's on

---

[3] Outstanding Novels in American Literature (1789–1959): *The Power of Sympathy* (1789) by Mrs. Sarah Wentworth Morton. *Wieland* (1789) by Charles Brockden Brown. *Charlotte Temple* (1790) by Susanna Haswell Rowson. *Modern Chivalry* (1792/3/7) by Hugh Henry Brackenridge. *The Algerine Captive* (1797) by Royall Tyler. *The Coquette* (1797) by Hannah Walker Foster. *Female Quixoticism* (1808) by Tabitha Tenny. *Randolph* (1823) by John Neal. *The Last of the Mohicans* (1826) and *Deerslayer* (1841) by James Fenimore Cooper. *The Dutchman's Fireside* (1831) by James Kirke Paulding. *The Infidel* (1835) by Albert Pike. *The Linwoods* (1835) by Catherine Maria Sedgewick. *George Balcombe* (1836) by Nathaniel Beverley Tucker. *Nick of the Woods* (1837) by Robert Montgomery Bird. *Zenobia* (1837) by William Ware. *The Green Mountain Boys* (1840) by Daniel Pierce Thompson. *Two Years Before the Mast* (1841) by Richard Henry Dana. *Margaret* (1845) by Sylvestre Judd. *Kaloolah* (1849) by

a stand beside him. *That's* his home away from home now, Chatauqua Moon wants him to know. He's not retiring! she says to him. Mick turns the platen knob clockwise and underlines "That's" for emphasis. "Too hip and thanks, Chat," Mick says into the mic Larry has set up. Mick digs Maxxis Grifter 20" x 1.85" tires, he says in between blasts from the keys. He's not about to retire. Too bad they don't make 88's, he adds. "Not yet, O'Grady!" Rodderick calls out. Chad "inTRIKat" Johnston laughs. Bonfire is happening. Cyclists ride through flames on the ghetto snake run made out of pallets and plywood that Genevieve Fennelseed helped build. Krylon spray paint crackles. VISION. Fennelseed's here with her girlfriend, Mick sees. Ms. Melvina? he wonders. Wonders about her. She's smiling. What a Babe. Mick backspaces and underlines Babe. He's running out of room on the page. Time to ride.

Schizoid is playing.

William Starbuck Mayo. *The Scarlet Letter* (1850), *The House of the Seven Gables* (1851), and *The Marble Faun* (1860) by Nathaniel Hawthorne. *Moby Dick* (1851) and *Billy Budd* (1891) by Herman Melville. *Uncle Tom's Cabin* (1852) by Harriet Beecher Stowe. *The Virginia Comedians* (1854) by John Esten Cooke. *Woodcraft* (1854) by William Gilmore Simms. *Elsie Venner* (1861) by Oliver Wendell Holmes. *John Brent* (1862) by Theodore Winthrop. *Hans Brinker* (1865) by Mary Mapes Dodge. *Little Women* (1868) by Louisa May Alcott. *The Hoosier Schoolmaster* (1871) by Edward Eggleston. *The Adventures of Tom Sawyer* (1876), *The Adventures of Huckleberry Finn* (1885), and *The Man That Corrupted Hadleyburg* (1900) by Mark Twain [Samuel L. Clemens]. *Miss Ravenal's Conversion from Secession to Loyalty* (1876) by John William De Forest. *A Fool's Errand* (1879) by Albion Winegar Tourgee. *Ben Hur* (1880) by Gen. Lew Wallace. *Washington Square* (1881) and *The Ambassadors* (1903) by Henry James. *The Story of a Country Town* (1883) by E. W. Howe. *Ramona* (1884) by Helen Hunt Jackson. *The Rise of Silas Lapham* (1885) by William Dean Howells. *East Angels* (1886) by Constance Fenimore Woolson.

Looking Backward (1888) by Edward Bellamy. *In the Valley* (1890) and *The Damnation of Theron Ware* (1896) by Harold Frederic. *Colonel Carter of Cartersville* (1891) by F. Hopkinson Smith. *The Cliff-Dwellers* (1893) by Henry Blake Fuller. *Maggie: A Girl of the Streets* (1893) and *The Red Badge of Courage* (1895) by Stephen Crane. *A Kentucky Cardinal* (1894) by James Lane Allen. *David Harum* (1898) by Edward Noyes Westcott. *When Knighthood Was in Flower* (1898) by Charles Major. *McTeague* (1899) by Frank Norris. *To Have and to Hold* (1899) by Mary Johnston. *Sister Carrie* (1900) and *An American Tragedy* (1925) by Theodore Dreiser. *The Virginian* (1902) by Owen Wister. *The Sea Wolf* (1904) by Jack London. *The Jungle* (1906) by Upton Sinclair. *Melanctha* (1909) and *The Making of Americans* (1925) by Gertrude Stein. *Ethan Frome* (1911) by Edith Wharton. *Westways* (1913) by Dr. Silas Weir Mitchell. *Penrod* (1914) and *Alice Adams* (1921) by Booth Tarkington. *The Harbor* (1915) by Ernest Poole. *My Antonia* (1918) by Willa Cather. *Jurgen* (1919) by James Branch Cabell. *Winesburg, Ohio* (1919) by Sherwood Anderson. *Main Street* (1920) and *Babbitt* (1922) by Sinclair Lewis. *The Great American Novel* (1923) by William Carlos Williams. *The Great Gatsby* (1925) by F. Scott Fitzgerald. *The Venetian Glass Nephew* (1925) by Elinor Wylie. *Early Autumn* (1926) and *The Rains Came* (1937) by Louis Bromfield. *Show Boat* (1926) and *Saratoga Trunk* (1941) by Edna Ferber. *The Bridge of San Luis Rey* (1927) by Thornton Wilder. *A Farewell to Arms* (1929) and *For Whom the Bell Tolls* (1940) by Ernest Hemingway. *Homeward Angel* (1929) and *You Can't Go Home Again* (1940) by Thomas Wolfe. *Sound and Fury* (1929) and *As I Lay Dying* (1930) by William Faulkner. *The Deepening Stream* (1930) by Dorothy Canfield Fisher. *Gone with the Wind* (1930) by Margaret Mitchell. *The Good Earth* (1931) by Pearl Buck. *Tobacco Road* (1932) by Erskine Caldwell. *Miss Lonelyhearts* (1933) and *The Day of the Locust* (1939) by Nathanael West. *Appointment in Samarra* (1934) by John O'Hara. *The Postman Always Rings Twice* (1934) by James M. Cain. *The Last Puritan* (1935) by George Santayana. *Studs Lonigan* (1935) by James T. Farrell. *Vein of Iron* (1935) and *The Woman Within* (1954) by Ellen Glasgow. *The Late George Apley* (1937) by John P. Marquand. *Northwest Passage* (1937) by Kenneth Roberts. *The Sea of Grass* (1937) and *The Town* (1950) by Conrad Richter. *U.S.A.* (1938) by John Dos Passos. *The Grapes of Wrath* (1939) by John Steinbeck. *Pale Horse, Pale Rider* (1939) by Katherine Anne Porter. *The Heart Is a Lonely Hunter* (1940) by Carson McCullers. *Native Son* (1940) by Richard Wright. *The Ox-bow Incident* (1940) by Walter Van Tilburg Clark. *The Journal of Albion Moonlight* (1941) by Kenneth Patchen. *The Fountainhead* (1943) by Ayn Rand. *The Human Comedy* (1943) by William Saroyan. *The Big Sky* (1947) and *The Way West* (1950) by A. B. Guthrie, Jr. *Trail from Needle Rock* (1947) by Peter Field. *Guard of Honor* (1948) by James Gould Cozzens. *The Naked and the Dead* (1948) by Norman Mailer. *Other Voices, Other Rooms* (1948) by Truman Capote. *The Young Lions* (1948) by Irwin Shaw. *Opus 21* (1949) and *The Disappearance* (1951) by Philip Wylie. *The Sheltering Sky* (1949) by Paul Bowles. *The Disenchanted* (1950) by Budd Schulberg. *The Wall* (1950) by John Hersey. *The Catcher in the Rye* (1951) by Jerome David Salinger. *From Here to Eternity* (1951) by James Jones. *Lie Down in Darkness* (1951) by William Styron. *The Invisible Man* (1952) by Ralph Ellison. *The Adventures of Augie March* (1953) by Saul Bellow. *The Bad Seed* (1954) by William March. *The Ponder Heart* (1954) by Eudora Welty. *Andersonville* (1955) by MacKinlay Kantor. *A Death in the Family* (1957) by James Agee. *On the Road* (1957) by Jack Kerouac. *Lolita* (1958) by Vladimir Nabokov. *Fade Out* (1959) by Douglas Woolf.

Is everybody in?
The ceremony is about to begin.

Number Forty-Four
Mike Daily

Number Forty-Three
Mat Hoffman

"A storm was rolling in as I was setting it up and right as I shot it it started pouring. It was cool."

Whiteski

Number Forty-Two
James White

```
YO
here's the thing I did
MOON BABES!

Thanks!
Willie D (ghetto Boys)
```

Number Forty-One
W. E. Dolney

My to-do list is so long, it's mind-boggling.

Number Forty
Ron W

What don't we know about that car?

Specifically that car... one second. [Pause.] The car, let's see. Well, it was just kind of doing like a dream kind of thing 'cause you know from street riding and everywhere you go—the tour, everything we did—the first thing we did was go street ridin'.

We'd get to where we traveled so much, we'd know places. Cities all over. Where to go ride. Or we'd just be familiar with the cities. And you know, that's kind of just a dream thing we'd always dream of is like ridin' on a car. Like, who hasn't dreamed about that? [Laughs.] And especially back then, it had never been done before. Never. It wasn't a thing. So it was cool in makin' the street contest just kind of like creating things that you'd find on the street as much as we could. The dirt bank-to-wall, which was something that you'd find on the street. Especially back then. Moreso than now as civilization has—quote—evolved. I think you don't see as many bank-to-walls as you once did. I remember San Diego had 'em all over the place. We'd go street ridin' and go from bank-to-wall to bank-to-wall. You'd have all choices. Like bank-to-gap-to-walls, bank-to-wall, curved bank-to-wall...you'd have all kinds of choices. There were so many and now, you don't see 'em anymore. Anyways, the car was just something you dream of doing. Finding an old car somewhere, ridin' around. It was cool to get it from a junkyard and paint it up and then just say, "OK you guys. Here you go. Put ramps up to it." [Laughs.] Lettin' people put the ramps where they want. The whole day was a completely groundbreaking kind of thing. The whole thing—the whole day—was surrealistic. You kind of get the vibe just from watchin' the videos. How it was just kind of like a cut-your-chains-off kind of thing. And that's exactly what it was. Well, I mean like what street riding did was just open up a whole new type of event. All the events up to that time were, like, contests. Showmanship and appearance. There was a lot of riders that aren't contest riders, they're just riders. And street riding kind of spoke to them to come and do their thing. It was a moment. Can't be recreated. [Laughs.] Ever.

How it was created seemed like totally on the fly. Didn't you have a last-minute date change so it wouldn't conflict with a contest that was happening or tours or something? How did you get the word out back then?

Yeah, that's another reason why it could never happen because—you know—nowadays of Internet and all that kind of stuff, it's so much different. Word of mouth. And that's really it. There was no Internet. And the magazines came out once a month. That whole thing just made the event that much more cool because all those people were there just from word of mouth. Just from word of mouth. Those days, we would send out flyers for a contest to all the magazines and the bike companies months in advance. I think three months was our scheduled time to send out flyers ahead of time. And always I'd be stressin' before then tryin' to get 'em done in time. Get 'em sent in time so they'd get there in time for the event. And people would make their plans. And then you have a date change and now that's a whole 'nother wrench. You'd have no idea if anyone's even gonna show up. Your friends are gonna show up but that's it. It's kind of cool. I mean, lookin' at the videos now and seein' it—in the videos from back then—it's like…uh…you can kind of… it brings back memories of the feeling of that day. Because it was such a groundbreaking moment in time for...for...BMX! [Laughs.] And the world. So you could say it was a moment in time in the world.

Didn't you have event insurance through Boy Scouts of America?

I don't know. Did we have insurance? I'm not sure if we did or not. And the funny thing is I just got permission from the store. I told 'em, "We'll have a little event here with a few friends. There's a bank there that people already ride. It's gonna be on a Sunday." They were like, "OK." And I don't even know if it was the manager. [Laughs.] And then all of a sudden, 500 people show up and ramps and cars! Spray paint. It was a pretty cool thing to have been at, and experience.

For sure. That's how it seems.

Everything about it was all unconventional. It was cool seein' the guys that weren't contest guys having a platform to show their skills. That was super cool. 'Cause a lot of the guys weren't guys you'd see in all the other contests. Guys that had been around.

Right. One guy that comes to mind is Jason Parkes.

Oh yeah. Jason Parkes. Yeah.

There's only one photo of him that got magazine coverage. Super BMX Freestyle and he's actually wall-riding the car. Did you see that?

Oh yeah. I do remember that. Yep. Yeah, he's one of those kind of guys. It's just a crack-up seeing the videos because that puts you right back in those times, and the feeling of the time. You can just see it. The way people are acting. Someone drinks a beer or something like that and it's like, "Oh. OK." At any other event that would be like a major, major deal. You know? Someone's drinkin' a beer. Here, it was like... this is it. People would try and do the normal things that would normally be like renegade/rebel things to do at an event and they just didn't fly. They just fell flat. Anything someone would try to do would just fall flat because the whole event was like that. Especially in those days. BMXers were completely outcasts or like different than all the rest of society. Entirely. You know?

Yeah.

There wasn't the big skate culture there is now. Even BMX as big as it is now, it wasn't like alternative things. There wasn't media like there is now. You know, you were a freak if you were in BMX. But then, once you organize an event—an organized event with judges and a contest with all these kind of guys—there's always gonna be guys that are tryin' to out-crazy the other guy. I remember seeing people at that event and it would just be like, "Oh." They wouldn't get the attention they were seeking because the event kind of overshadowed it. The street riding and just the free-for-allness of it.

Do you remember who painted the car? Grasso obviously...

Yeah, it was a combination of people. I tried to control it a little bit but then people started bringing cans and spraying. There were a couple guys that were better at it than others and they're usually the ones that take over.

Obviously that car was demolished at the end of the contest. Do you remember how you disposed of it?

I think we made a deal with a junkyard like at our other street events. They would bring it out and we'd wreck it and they'd come get it. And then also we'd have to make sure—we'd always <u>try</u> and make sure—people wouldn't pop the tires because they'd have to tow it away. I remember stressin' about that at certain street contests. It'd always get to a point to where all of a sudden there's like four guys that are on the car like bashin' on it and releasing massive amounts of pent-up destruction inside of them. I'd go over there to make sure no one popped the tires. We put blocks of wood under the tires so when you jumped on the car it wouldn't bounce so much. Old school American cars. The shocks aren't very sturdy in those things.

How do you feel about the Ron Wilkerson Appreciation Page that's up on Facebook?

I haven't even ever seen it.

Really?

That's cool. Over the years, I heard there's a couple and people would update 'em regularly. Super cool. I just don't do any of that shit—social media stuff—whatsoever. None. Zero. Zilch. I do entertain it at times with all the stuff I want to do like makin' a book. That's how you get the word out for things. And then I just say, "Well, I'll get all my friends to put it on their pages." When I'm done with work, I don't wanna look at a computer. And then the whole thing too—Instagram—I'm like, "I'm way too busy living my life to take pictures of it and have it for someone else." Like, fuck that.

I admire that.

When I'm doin' something, I'm in the moment. I'm not takin' pictures of it for another moment. Or for some other person. I'm in the moment. Just there for me and people I'm with. That's my whole thing. How many times have you been with people that want to take pictures of everything? People that put the stuff up right away. It's like, "Are you even here? Am I with you? Or are you over there with all those other people?" Like, God. "Where is your conscience at?" The reality is it's our current society. Living like that. It's how our current society lives and nearly everyone in it. And it's like…I'm just… not me. People who know me, they know what I'm up to. I could have the bombest Instagram page ever in this universe. With all the places I've been to even in the last year. Stuff I've experienced.

Admirable, man.

And besides that, you know, I like to go places. A whole 'nother facet of that is like when I go somewhere, I don't want the world knowing where I am. I don't want anyone knowing that. I just want to be there myself with whoever I'm with and experience it. Why do I want everyone to know where I am?

Yeah.

I don't knock anybody for that. That's fine. Go. Go crazy. Whatever makes you happy. Just not me. Just don't push me into it. And that…that…it's funny that we're talking about this right now—what we just talked about—that was the big part of me steppin' off the treadmill for 2-Hip and changin' my focus, was that to succeed in a business like that, it's all about your web presence and your social media presence. That's the only way you can do it. I mean, there's not even any magazines anymore. That's all it is. And it's like…I'm just like, you know…if I have this business for 25 years or more then all of a sudden I gotta turn into that guy, to keep it going? I gotta be that guy to keep it going? Fuck that. Fuck that. I'm outta here.

"It was a killer project to create and glad we did. That 'Doba is too cool. Stoked I got to do it."
-Fetus

Number Thirty-Nine
Patrick Richardson

Roots Art by Craig Grasso

Number Thirty-Eight (Four Thousand Three Hundred Forty-Three)

Maurice Meyer

"After four years of competing in AFA contests, it became obvious it was time to step back. Riders were comping-up hard ready to stomp some pros, my tricks were feeling dated, 'practicing' was starting to suck, the industry was tanking bad and basically it was time to get a job. Not the best of transitions to go from the buzz of being in the golden years of such an awesome thing as BMX freestyle, but these occasional mentions in the magazine helped soften the blow big time. It sure is nice to be missed.

The mustache has become somewhat legendary. I don't know why. Hugo and Woody both had them and Hugo's was way more substantial than mine. Years later someone asked online why we both had them so I replied: 'Hugo and I both had a mustache clause in our contracts. Skyway wanted us to present an air of virility. So we did.' Really though: I had mine to try to appear older and maybe transition into a team manager job or something. That and maybe the fact that all four of my brothers still at home had them. So I did."

A no-show for Drob in Bristol, but once again .. he would've been stoked if he'd have shown up.

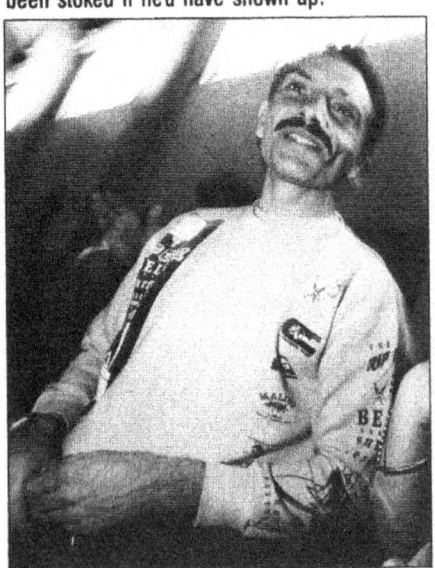

Maurice Meyer wasn't there, but he would've been stoked if he'd have shown up.

GUEST REPLY

GO,
 What's the deal with the constant mentionings and hidden photos of Maurice Meyer? It always brings a smile to my face, but tell me WHY?

David Kent
Export, Pennsylvania

David — why don't we let Maurice himself answer your question. Drob?

The temptation of big money brought in riders from everywhere. Everywhere but San Francisco, that is . . .

RORY LUCAS

"**Easter Egg**" in *The Birth of the Freestyle Movement* (2017, First Edition)
and *The Birth of the BMX Freestyle Movement* (2019, Second Edition)

2-HIP PROMOTIONS
P.O. 4065
LEUCADIA CA 92024
619-753-7697

King of Vert

Dear Spike, LOU, and Andy,
Just needing to send a note to comment on the legacy you 3 have left in the BMXworld - and please allowme to call youTThe Trinity - as there were always many different BMX mags coming or going, but there was only ONE BMX Freestyle Bible, Freestylin' Magazine, created by The Trinity...BEFORE the days you would see a video worldwide within minutes of a groundbreaking new trick being pulled for the first time...BEFORE there were these little 'webpedit' thingys everywhere...BEFORE video asa form of communication even frickin' EXISTED.

There were only magazines. Once a month.

Freestylin' Magazine existed for riders during a time when magazines were your LIFELINE, your CONNECTION, your INSPIRATION. The power each issue of that mag did wield will never again in HISTORY exist in that same concentr8ed form as it did for us riders as Freestylin' Mag did then. EACH RIDER would look forward to each month when the mailman would come with the next issue, and then we'd POUR over every mm of the book, breathing it in, swallowing it, trying to emul8 the influence, ridàng or otherwise, until the next issue.

Freestylin' Mag didn't just "cover BMX"(the detrimental folly of OTHER BMX magazines), the unique way it feathred ALLof the gr8 variety of riders and styles, capturing each's OWN uniqueness, actually played a big part in CREATING BMX Freestyle. Granted it was a grand time for creativity in the UNIVERSE, in BMX Freestyle or otherwise, birthing Punk Rock, birthing computers, barthing digital manipulations, and it WAS only a magazine, but you guys created BMXX Freestyle just as importantly as the guys who created it created it, enhancïng the LIFESTYLE... And being 'one of those guys', i can say that your collective genius in glossy print form did TRANSFORM the 2D page, effecting the rider to KNOW they were involved in something extraordinary, as the uniqueness of each Freestylin' issue did actually MATCH the uniqueness that did exist in BMX Freestyle.

You tri-handedly(Trinity)represented BMX in a way that influenced lives, the residual still in effect to this DAY, as hordes of riders have continued in their lives remaining effected now BECAUSE OF HOW THEY WERE INFLUENCED THEN! Foreals, during that time you helped make us ALL so proud to be involved in something so cool as BMX Freestyle, which ENHANCED our own personàlities, and even made SOME OF US motiv8ed to continue that feeling by making EVENTS that captured that same Energy of making riders feel PROUD to be into BMX. (Thats how exponential progress works.)
Let me just sayin closing, with surety, that thanx to you 3, The Trinity, and thanx to OZ, If there was never such a thing as Freestylin' Mag, BMX Freestyle would never have impacted as many lives as it has done in such a MASSIVE way. You DEFINED coolness for an entire generation.
Regards,
Ron W (AKA ROn Wilkerson.)

W E   R I D E - W E   A R E   H I P

Number Thirty-Seven
Dominic Phipps

MD: "There were only magazines. Once a month."
—Ron Wilkerson to Spike Jonze, Mark Lewman, and Andy Jenkins

That letter. Typewritten. What year was that?

DP: The letter was written specifically for the book. I have the original here. Ron wanted to express his love and thanks to those guys. Not sure of his claims on dates being correct.

Oh wow. I thought it was an artifact. Couldn't place the era. That explains why! It reads with the energy and brilliance that Oz always exhibited.

Yeah it was an idea for a while. Ron was really into it. Then literally the day before I went to print he still hadn't written it. He asked me for two more days. I said "no cigar"—I need it tonight. He rode his bike to a thrift store in Santa Cruz, bought a typewriter and knocked it out in the early hours of the morning. Ron is a dude for all seasons.

That's a story that should be the nucleus of a feature article. Representative of everything the book entails.

Good call. I wish I had more time to do more. There's a lot of behind the scenes stuff to share. Ron sent this when he was typing the letter.

Great documentation image. I know the feeling having no time. Well if you don't mind I'd like to be #1 on the list for possibly writing about that for you.

Yeah absolutely. I'd be delighted. I have a film crew coming to the launch. There was some interest in a doc series from a studio. Making a short teaser reel. I'm not getting my hopes high, but it could be another place to get this culture, story, community some recognition. So I guess I'll keep campaigning. Great story. Remarkable people. It needs to be celebrated.

I'm only on page 80 and I'm celebrating. Incredible time machine, your book. I hope the film crew recognizes its potential.

Thanks Mike.

Number Thirty-Six
Ron Lesniewski

Number Thirty-Five
Jeffrey Cousineau

Number Thirty-Four
Andy Werth

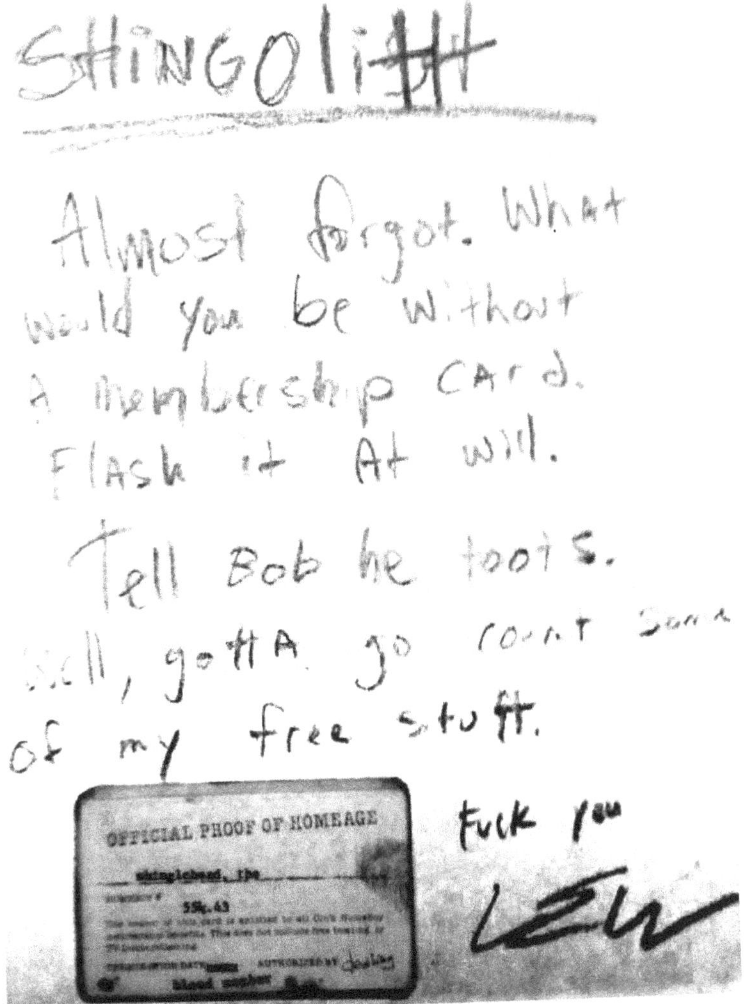

SHiNGOli ~~||||~~

Almost forgot. What would you be without a membership card. Flash it at will.

Tell Bob he toots.

Well, gotta go count some of my free stuff.

Fuck you

OFFICIAL PROOF OF HOMEAGE

Number Thirty-Three
Jeff Venekamp

SPIKE JONZE

"Photo is from a slide Spike sent me back in 1988."
—Ryan Schierling,
Monkey Meets The Blowtorch

Number Thirty-One — Steev Inge
HOW TO iLLUSTRATE THE iLLEST RiDES!

1. make rad friends
2. Take Pictures
3. Draw Bikes for 30 years.
4. get so stoked you spend days perfecting your favorite rad ride ever.
5. make into stickers and tshirts to share the stoke

POORBOYSteev moon babes club member #31

Cherrypicker.
Photo by Rob Smith

Number Thirty
Matt Bass

Number Twenty-Nine
Andy Bullock

As a kid bikes were not just about getting around. Sure I did ride my bike everywhere in San Jose. Once a friend of my parents told them they had seen me by the Fairgrounds (I was

9 years old and that was about 8 miles from my house). They didn't believe it.

It was true.

There were some badass gully jumps near a railroad underpass right by there. One right near the tracks had a bump near the top that if you hit it right with enough speed you could do almost do a tabletop.

It was also about taking what you had and customizing it. The crap bike became cooler with different cranks, a Tuf-Neck and some mags. I wish I had some pictures of my first proper BMX bike, but I have these, the first bike. Heavy as an anchor. I broke the frame shortly after the second photo was taken.

When I moved south to Santa Ana it became bigger bikes, 26" cruisers with BMX parts then eventually building death traps like hill bomb sidehacks with no cranks out of Schwinn Scramblers. Then skateboarding, when bikes became the way to get to the ditch. But when we started to ride Pipeline in Upland because of my BMX

roots, I occasionally would borrow a bike to take rides in the full pipe. And when I went to school in Vegas the cultures mixed completely. We would pile bikes and boards into cars and go ride.

Number Twenty-Seven
Eric Buxton

Number Twenty-Six
Adam Levi Hungate (Guitar God)

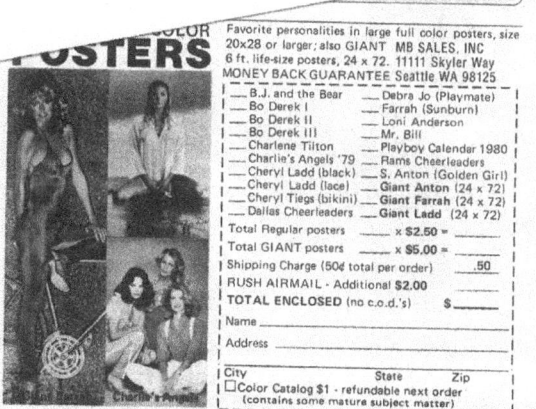

Number Twenty-Five
Steve Brothers

There's a lot of interesting projects currently afoot, which are being produced by our fellow BMXers. I just wanted to mention how important I believe it is that we support these things. Most of us would concede that we like to support BMX culture. But what does that mean? It can be as simple as "liking" a post, but often it entails more—supporting a project monetarily.

We are fortunate as rarely do these projects exceed $50... supporting some of these endeavors is a fraction of that. But sometimes the organizers, authors, musicians —the people driving these efforts—have to invest a fair amount to make these projects happen. My point here is that we should support that.

You may not love everything about a given project, but I urge people to consider supporting in principle.

What the hell am I talking about, some may be wondering? I'm talking about a broad swath of projects, including varying types—books, zines, music projects, podcasts, art projects and certainly also events.

Don't hit people up for free copies or free tickets or registrations. Don't try to get by doing as little as you can. Support these things to the fullest of your capacity. We all have limited budgets, so we can't all be in on everything—but the support threshold could be a lot higher on things. I urge folks to consider it.

There's great podcasts too. Rail the Berm has some great episodes. There's a number of other great podcasts too. Check them out. "Like" them. Share them. That's legit support.

I'm hemorrhaging funds in the lead up to the show, but when I see Haro & Andy doing a music project, when I see 44:16 Zine for a mere $5 bucks running articles on BMX culture, or Mike Daily from the Plywood Hoods launching a new book with the coolest most creative "perks"... I want to support that. I want these guys to know the effort is appreciated and the work is respected. It doesn't matter really that I've never been an 80's synth music connoisseur, but I want these guys to do their thing and I support it. When Dom Phipps is promoting his latest book, The Birth of the BMX Freestyle Movement, I want to amplify that opportunity so people know this book is available. Plus, doing so only edifies us…we learn we understand more about our sport.

I get that none of us are made of money… but if you really can't support financially at least show some love and respond by liking or sharing the social media posts for these events. Sometimes it feels like the Old School BMX Community has never really understood what it is to be a community. It means mutual support. Sometimes we do so in principle regardless of whether it's our particular niche.

Gotta have a pic with the post or far fewer people will read it. So I grabbed a bunch of BMX project wares that I had immediately at hand. I have a number of Mike Daily books here, Joe Pernice (old school collector) books and I have a bunch of his Scud Mountain Boys and Pernice Bros. CD's too. GJS project supporting the senior dog rescue, the 44:16 zine I just recently got and BMX Society event poster. These are the sorts of projects that I see value in. I hope the community will too.

Number Twenty-Four
Ethan Lundquist

Number Twenty-Three
Rich Bartlett

SMILEY ROY

Number Twenty-Two
Roy de Guzman

Number Twenty-One
Adam Fleetwood

Number Twenty
Josh Smith

HOMETOWN: Originally from Pekin, Illinois (if you cross the bridge of Peoria, you're not far)

BIKE(S) CURRENTLY USED: My recent acquisitions are a 19 inch Haro Master (the limited Red one-ALWAYS wanted one), and the 19.5 Yellow Master (almost finished putting it together!)

MAJOR ACCOMPLISHMENTS IN FREESTYLE: Hmmmm. I guess that I still have an interest since 1984? I may not ride every day, but I still love this sport, and try to find ways to contribute to it when I can.

PAST SPONSORS: Mom, Dad, both step parents, Aunt Shirley (rest in peace), the Pekin Daily Times paper route, the Journal Star paper route, Long John Silvers, Wendy's and The Army National Guard/Air Force.

FAVORITE RIDING AREA: Generally any decent parking lot will do.

NON-BMX HEROES: Eddie Van Halen, Mark Hamill, JJ Abrams, Damon Johnson, Salvador Dali.

HOBBIES: (OTHER THAN RIDING) I mess with several of my guitars. I'm a huge Star Wars fan. I love comics and reading books. I also volunteer my time as a member of the 501st Legion

GIRLFRIEND/WIFE: I'm currently engaged to my longtime partner, Jennifer Wiggins. We are talking about tying the knot possibly next summer?

Allan McNaughton and Sandy Carson
Photographer: Ricky Adam

Number Nineteen
Allan McNaughton

... somehow evokes the view from a teenage bedroom in some Scottish new town circa 1982 at the same time as a modern mall food court in modern-day San Francisco? Tightly wound sounds formed in the nucleus of UKDIY and the post-JAM mod revival - MAXIMUMROCKNROLL

neutrals.bandcamp.com

Number Eighteen
Manuel Juan Rios

 greaserbmxer Man i have not looked forward to something like this in awhile... so new, different reminds me of the beginnings of bmx freestyle 🙌🔥🔥 a cross between hunter s. Thomson and eminem freestylin about things only those that know.... know 🙌

10w   1 like   Reply

Number Seventeen
Matt Picker

"Even though riding naked was my downfall, it was positive at the same time and made me push on and not give a shit what people thought."
— Craig Grasso

"Finding Grasso: Part 3"
Published on Sep 24, 2018

Number Sixteen
Brian Tunney

"In the late 1980s, Craig Grasso was at the forefront of a growing movement within the BMX scene towards a new form of riding: street riding. Instead of adhering to strictly ramps or flatland, Grasso was one of the first riders to gain exposure through free riding the streets around where he lived in Redondo Beach, California. With the Wizard Publications office a town away in Torrance, the photographers from both Freestylin' and BMX Action gravitated towards Grasso's riding, style of dress and antics. Many of his original moves were captured in the magazines before he abruptly disappeared from the BMX scene. 'Finding Grasso' is an attempt to look back at his influence on BMX. This is part 3, from the crow-ridden area of Hermosa Beach."

—Brian Tunney

The Oregonian

The Oregonian/BRENT WOJAHN

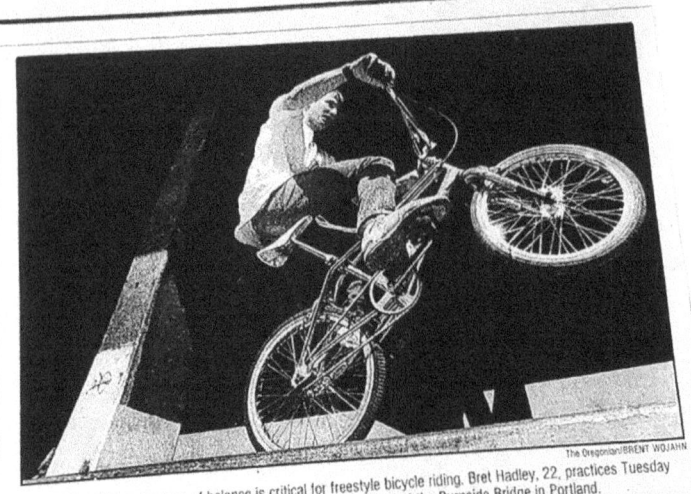

Freewheeling: A sense of balance is critical for freestyle bicycle riding. Bret Hadley, 22, practices Tuesday in an area set aside for skaters and others beneath the east end of the Burnside Bridge in Portland.

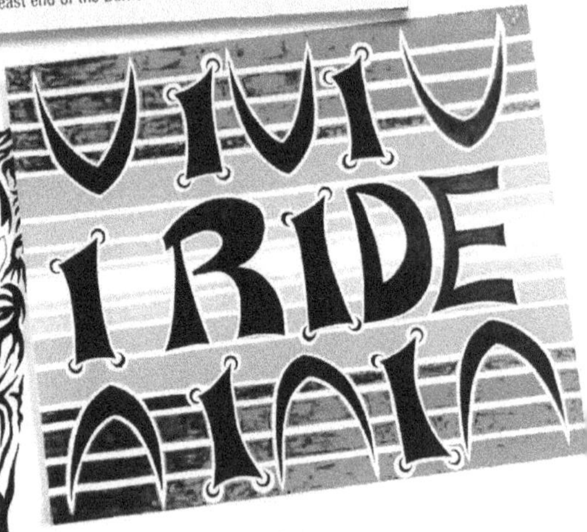

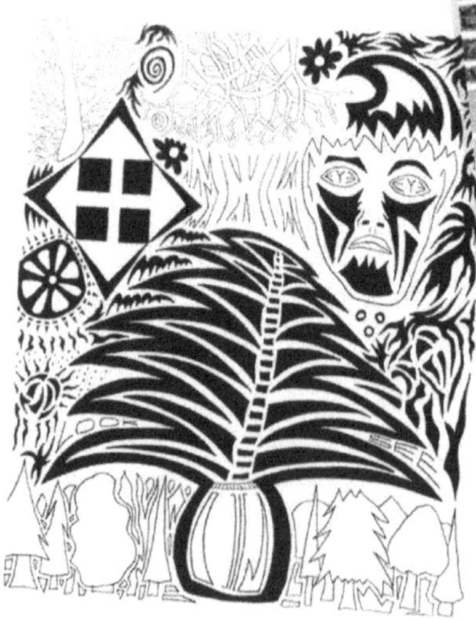

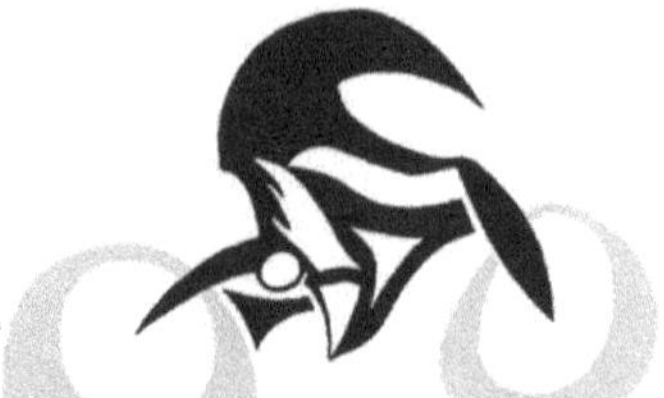

Number Fifteen

Bret Hadley

Number Fourteen
Mike McCormick

Photo: Tony McCormick

Number Thirteen
Wes Barnett
"I had a dream I learned brakeless decades.
A symbol of some sort?"

Number Twelve
Don Amundson

Number Eleven
Jerry Loera

Number Ten
Luke Strahota

Number Nine
Don Grzelak

I guess first of all I've always loved Ceppie Maes' CW since seeing it in the magazines as a teenager. It almost looked kind of basic compared to what was out there at the time, but when you looked closer at it, it was just so cool. The drum brake hubs being the main thing that was pretty amazing to me.

Skip to about 15 years later. I had moved to Indiana from Chicago and been out here about two years and ended up getting a house. There was this one wall I decided I wanted to decorate with every color of the CW double crossbar freestyle bars. I started looking for and buying them on eBay, which until then I was just using that site to buy Star Wars and old monster toys.

I ended up buying a set of black bars from a guy named Lou in Florida. He wrote me and told me he was working on building a Ceppie bike and those were from it, and he asked if I was interested in buying the rest of the bike he was working on. That sounded awesome and I ended up getting it. It was really cool, but it wasn't exactly the same as Ceppie's. It was a different CW California Freestyle frame, it had a drum brake wheelset (but not Sturmey Archer drums and different rims), and CW double crossbar bars of course that I was buying in the first place instead of the ones with the single crossbar. It was awesome stuff, just not exactly his bike. Lou ended up telling me about the Vintage BMX website and mentioned that there was a lot of us on there that were into the old bikes. I ended up checking it out and it was awesome.

As I was getting more into collecting bikes and parts, I decided I wanted to build the Ceppie bike up how I knew it. As I was looking more into it, I realized there were some different parts on it from time to time—I'm sure as something broke or wore out and got replaced—but I ended up finding one picture and decided to go off of that. It was the two-page fold-out from the July 1986 BMX Action how-to section of him doing a trick.

Here's what I wrote on my BMX Museum entry for it:

"Was going for a bike like the one Ceppie rode in the how-to/interview in the July 1986 BMX Action. Thanks to everyone who sent me pix of him riding for reference. You'd be surprised how many little differences there were between his bikes in lots of the pix. Anyway, here's my tribute to Ceppie Maes."

- Frame/Fork: CW
- Bars: CW Freestyle
- Sturmey-Archer Drum Brake hubs
- MKS pedals
- Comp ST tires
- ACS Z-rims
- Skyway Spinmaster
- ACS levers
- A'me grips
- Shotgun II seat
- Seat Post: Uni

Here's the pic that was my main focus for the bike.

That picture didn't show everything perfect, but it was pretty good. I ended up collecting parts to start. I kind of like for parts to have their original finish these days, but at that time I wasn't against refinishing something to be the color I needed. I ended up finding a painted frame that was blue fading into white that was pretty beat up, forks that were spray-painted silver, a blue seat, green bars, a blue seatpost, silver cranks. A friend of mine in Chicago let me know that he had a friend who powdercoated a lot of fences and stuff for the city, and if I ever needed anything black to let him know and he could have that done for me. This

was kind of a perfect project for that so I let him know what I had in mind. He's an old freestyler too, so he was all into it. I ended up sending him the big box of stuff, and it eventually came back to me all shiny black. A nice job too, I was really happy with it. Still am!

I ended up getting a blue seat that was exactly the one I needed, just not black. There was a thread on the Vintage site on dying certain plastic and rubber parts and I tried it out. Boiled a bunch of water, put it all in a bucket with some black Rit dye, waited a little while, and I had a black seat.

A set of black NOS Z-rims came up for sale on the site and I ended up picking those up. The hardest parts that took me the longest ended up being the hubs and the sticker set. I can get to the sticker set later, but in all the time that I was looking for the hubs I never found any at all for sale. You'd think you could find anything, but I was searching multiple sites many times a day and I never saw any come up at all. Finally one day I came across a bike shop in France that had some. There were Sturmey Archer hubs out there, just not these exact ones. I was so happy, finally the rear hub that took a single freewheel and not built for the multiple gears like on a road bike. I ended up ordering them. They were so cool when they got there. They were either new or NOS, I couldn't tell, but they were exactly what I wanted. Realizing that I had only ever laced up one wheelset—and that was OK, but not perfect—I brought these to a local bike shop in Fort Wayne and had them built up right. The guys at the bike shop thought it was pretty cool to see an NOS set of old black Z-rims and these hubs come in to the shop. Some of those guys were old BMXers too and they would sometimes take in old trade-ins for new bikes, and they'd show me the cool old ones they got in when I'd stop by. I remember the coolest being an old Patterson Cruiser one time.

By now, I think the only parts still being used from the first black CW were the black NOS Comp ST tires and the black Tuf-Neck chainring/power-disc combo. I ended up picking up an NOS Skyway Spinmaster that was still in the package, and some bubble font A'me Tri girps. There were some pictures of the bike with black and pink A'Me Unitron grips and

they looked awesome on there, but that main photo I was going off of had black A'me Tri grips on it, so I went with those. I picked up a set of used MKS graphite pedals and funny enough one of the caps on the end of the pedal was missing, broken off, just like in the photo. I probably wouldn't have gone that far to take the end cap off of one of the pedals just to match, but what I picked up for it matched, and I was ok with that.

By the time I had the wheels built up, I pretty much had all the parts, but still after a long time of searching many times a day I have never ran across a sticker set or even one single sticker like the set on his black and pink bike. I realized I had to take things into my own hands at this point. There were a few guys on the BMX sites that were making stickers and I got to talking to one of them about what I needed. He said he didn't have any, but if I could get him some artwork for them that he could make them. So I got to work on that.

I did have one single real CW fork sticker. Not black and pink, or even for this model, but I had a sticker with stripes on it and I went from there.

Online I came across a photo or scan of a set of CW frame stickers. I ended up downloading that picture, measuring my original fork sticker, then re-sizing the picture of the sticker set that I found in Photoshop to have its fork sticker match the size of my fork sticker. Once I did that, the rest of the stickers in that pic went to the scale that they needed to be. From there I just traced over what was there to make everything crisp lines. I was able to figure out the fonts that I needed for some of the words, and I just drew my own big block letters for some.

I was able to figure out everything except the word "California" for the top crossbar sticker. It's pretty funny how I got that. I either knew in the back of my mind somehow, or saw it recently at the time, but it reminded me of the California Raisins claymation ads years before so I looked that up. Yep, that was it. I'm sure it's a font, but I couldn't figure out which one, so I found a California Raisins ad, downloaded it, and traced over the word "Caifornia" in it. I put it all together and my sticker set was done. At least on the computer. I got in touch with the one making the stickers, asked what format would be best to get them to him, and sent them off. In the meantime, I printed off a paper set and taped them around the bike as a mock-up. I found an old pic of the bike with that taped paper on it while I was waiting for my real set to get here. The stickers were the final piece.

I'm pretty sure Ceppie welded his own pegs on his frame and forks, but I didn't have a way to do that, so mine is just a stock frame and stock Spinner forks that CW used with the screw-in pegs.

I think I finished it nine years ago now. I still have it, totally unchanged from the day I finished it. This is the bike I put the most work into as far as tracking down, some re-finishing, making my own artwork for it, and figuring out all the parts. I've had people want to buy it from me too but I know I'll be keeping this one.

There were a lot of awesome bikes that were around at the time, but only one had me wanting to put this much work into trying to see it in person. And this was the one.

Number Eight
Erik Matsunaga

Yes, that's me circa 1983.

I'd like to say I was 360'ing the hood of a Chrysler Cordoba, but it was a Universal Studios pic. You might see there is no left pedal. My foot was resting on a bar extending from the moon to the bottom bracket tube, a sort of a precursor to the Diamond Back diving board trick ad.

I was so stoked to sit on a Kuwahara. The year before I had bought a used Team Murray from my cousin, who thought it was a Red Line because he had bought it used from a kid who had put Red Line stickers on it and duped him.

But this was no Murray with Kuwahara stickers, this was the real deal, minus a left crank and pedal anyway.

Number Seven
Ross Lavender

"Here's me doing a half lash in the late eighties. Can't remember the year. Man, I miss that bike and I miss those days of riding without a care in the world. Started riding again 2 years ago and can't wait until my next session."

Number Six
Johnny Nolan

Number Five
Mike Sarris

How-to: The Miami Stopper

To do this trick, you need a locking front brake lever and your handlebars and seat must touch. You also need to be able to do a regular Miami Hopper. If you're running 990's on the chain stays, a bit of grip tape will need to be on your seat stays to keep your feet from sliding down (I rest my toes on the brake pads).

Step 1: Do a regular Miami Hopper. Lock your front brake, and rise up into a no-handed Miami Hopper.

Step 2: Remove your right foot from the pedal.

Step 3: Once you have your balance, move your right foot up to the rear peg. Place your toes on the seat stay and the center of your foot on the back peg.

Step 4: Get the back tire in the crack of your butt, and move your left foot up to the rear peg. Place your toes on the seat stay and the center of your foot on the back peg.

NBL Freestyle Series National 1990 Flatland 18 & Over Novice 1st Place

Step 5: When you have your balance again, slowly stand up by bending both knees at the same time to maintain your balance. This (and coming back down) is the hardest part.
Keep your knees slightly bent to assist in keeping your balance. Once you stand up, rest for a few seconds and wave to the crowd.

Step 6: When it's time to come down, slowly bend both knees until you're sitting on the back tire again. Move your left foot back to the pedal, then the right. Bend down and pull out of it as you would a regular Miami Hopper.

If you lose your balance while standing up or coming down, jump to the right while shoving the pegs to the left. I've never hurt myself bailing out like this.

If you pull it off, congratulations, you've done the craziest variation of the Miami Hopper. So far only three people have done it completely, and a young boy in Japan has stood up on the rear pegs. Will you be next?

Space Brothers PodcastPro Unlimited
Orlando, United States

A podcast covering all things BMX related, photography, art, design, space, nutrition, and many other topics hosted by Kip Williamson and co-host Chip Riggs.

Episode 43 - Chad Johnston
Episode 42 - Simon Tabron
Episode 41 - Dizz Hicks
Episode 40 - Rob Nolli
Episode 39 - Catfish
Episode 38 - Chad Kagy
Episode 37 - Voodoo Jam Recap
Episode 36 - Matt Beringer
Episode 35 - Nina Buitrago
Episode 34 - Sean Burns
Episode 33 - Art Thomason
Episode 32 - Fuzzy Hall
Episode 31 - John Buultjens
Episode 30 - Bill Nitschke
Episode 29 - Joe Johnson
Episode 28 - Swampfest Recap
Episode 27 - Mark Mulville
Episode 26 - Chase Gouin
Episode 25 - Brian Fox
Episode 24 - Steve Crandall
Episode 23 - Tim Knoll
Episode 22 - Rich Bartlett

Episode 21 - Scotty Cranmer
Episode 20 - Mark Eaton
Episode 19 - Mike Parenti
Episode 18 - Eddie Fiola
Episode 17 - Dave Brumlow
Episode 16 - Terry Adams
Episode 15 - Matt Coplon
Episode 14 - Scott Towne
Episode 13 - BMX Bros. Trey & Jabe Jones
Episode 12 - Marcos De Jesus
Episode 11 - X Games Shakedown
Episode 10 - BMX Trickstars
Episode 9 - Trey Jones
Episode 8 - Aaron Behnke
Episode 7 - Jam Circle
Episode 6 - Dave Voelker
Episode 5 - Ryan Sher
Episode 4 - Pete Augustin
Episode 3 - Chad DeGroot
Episode 2 - Ron Bonner
Episode 1 - Chip Riggs

All episodes are available now for free on ITunes, Spotify, Google Play, Stitcher, and SoundCloud by searching **"Space Brothers Podcast"** or you can visit **spacebrotherspodcast.com** and listen without downloading an app with any smartphone or computer.

Episode 20 - Mark Eaton

Shortly after the boom of BMX freestyle in the mid 80s, flatland changed seemingly overnight with a barrage of never before seen rolling tricks which changed the sport forever.

At a time when balancing and hopping tricks ruled the scene, and most sponsored riders lived in sunny CA, a group of young up and comers known as the Plywood Hoods from York PA were hungry to make a name for themselves. Little did most people know at the time, the Hoods were a well rounded group of riders who did it all. From BMX racing to riding skateparks, dirt jumps, and quarter pipes, they could hold their own. But where they really stood out, was flatland.

Mark Eaton was a cornerstone of the group who not only brought original rolling tricks to the masses like the whiplash and steam roller, but he also began recording every move the Plywood Hoods would take over the next 20 years creating 10 different videos known as the *Dorkin' In York* video series.

Every time they showed up to a contest all eyes were on them with video cameras aimed in their direction hoping to capture the next ground breaking trick. Even the top pros at the time kept their eyes on Mark, Kevin, and the other Plywood Hoods hoping to see something new they could add to their bag of tricks.

As the Plywood Hoods increased in popularity through magazine coverage and sponsor recognition, each video release became more popular. Mark continued evolving his riding skills and his talents in the video production world simultaneously. Each time a new *Dorkin'* video was released, not only did the riding get better but the quality improved along with it. Eventually Mark took his own riding down a new path and started incorporating flatland with street riding and pushed BMX in yet another direction. The Dorks from York showed they were some of the most talented and progressive riders in the world!

We sat down with Mark at the Master Blaster Planet Studios and discussed the first time he met Kevin Jones, how he almost gave up riding BMX in favor of breakdancing, coming up with original rolling tricks nobody had ever seen before, creating the *Dorkin' In York* video series, changing up his own personal riding style over the years, video and production work including several top-notch BMX titles such as *Joe Kid On A Sting-Ray: The History of BMX*, *Stompin' Stu*, and Mongoose *Know Your Roots* documentaries, and his current projects including a DJing career and doing video production for Penn State University.

So get comfortable, crank up your speakers, and get to know one of the most progressive BMX riders on two wheels, it's BMX legend, Mark Eaton!

—**Space Bros.**

Who was your first BMX hero, Mike?

Number Three
Bill Bunting

There were these three kids in my neighborhood that I kinda looked up to. Dan Mutter. Everyone called him Mut. Mike Fernandez. Everyone called him Fernie. And Kevin Goodall. He didn't have a nickname. Everyone just called him Goodall.

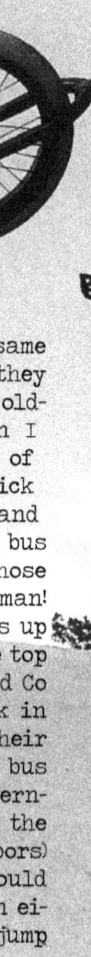

I guess when you go by your last name you don't need a nickname. We went to the same elementary school and they were a couple of years older. Like 6th grade when I was in 4th. That sort of thing. They would pick on me and my friends and throw rocks at us at the bus stop. That sucked. But those assholes could jump, man! The school bus picked us up at this vacant lot at the top of my street. Goodall and Co had built a little track in the lot and would ride their bikes right up until the bus got there. Goodall and Fernie lived right across the street (next door neighbors) from the bus stop and would just ditch their bikes in either garage and then jump on the bus, immediately going and sitting in the very back where the cool kids sat. They weren't always mean, Mutter was particularly nice when not in the presence of his two other stooges, and sometimes we'd ride together around the neighborhood. It was a developing neighborhood back then, so we built a few different tracks and jumping spots in the various dirt lots that were scattered throughout the area. Kinda like the neighborhood in E.T. but not as rich. Same time frame, too. Maybe a couple years earlier. Anyway, like I said earlier, these dudes could jump. High and far. And stylish. I don't remember any one handers or one footed table tops or

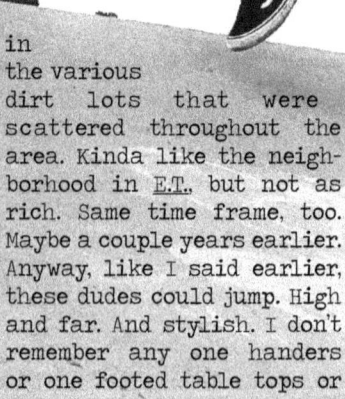

anything like that, but they ripped. And the three of them had really cool looking Mongeese. Mut's was red with Motomags. Fernie's was blue with Motomags. Goodall had the coolest one. Chrome with red pads and with a red Comp II on the front and a red snakebelly on the back. Black Tuffs. That bike kicked ass! Goodall's older brother Mike didn't BMX with us, but he could ride wheelies on his 10 speed forever. Just go and go around all the neighborhood blocks, only setting the front wheel down if he wanted to. So, those dudes were first. Then it was probably Harry Leary and Eddie King. The Diamond Back days. Harry's JMC days and Eddie's Torker days were about a year or so before I got hipped to the whole thing. I loved Diamond Back at the time and those guys were the shit, I thought. But my real first BMX hero was Andy Patterson. I thought Skyway ruled.

Or at least I thought Tuffs ruled. I didn't really care one way or the other about the TA at the time. Oh, and their jerseys and hats were cool. One time Andy Patterson came to our track. The PAL (Police Athletic League) Roadrunner BMX track. Early 82. I don't think he was Pro yet because we sure as hell didn't have a Pro class at our track and I remember that he entered and raced. Probably entered 16 Expert or something like that. Totally stomped the comp. Did all those awesome Andy Patterson jumps. Flat tables, one footers, 360s, etc. Styled hard. The next day he did a one man demo, with no ramps or anything, in a Burger King parking lot.

The handful of us kids that went just kinda watched him do 180 bunnyhops and 360 bunnyhops and that thing where you jump over the handlebars and sit on the crossbar while rolling forward and so on. We followed him around the parking lot and did curb endos and less impressive bunnyhops of our own, etc. He was really nice to all of us and exuded that California cool that exemplified BMX at the time. Checkered Vans and all. So I consider him to be my actual first BMX hero. There's been a lot more since then. So, yeah. Who was yours?

Number Two
Chris Reilly

Cathleen Kennedy-Reilly

Number One
Matt D'Angelo

HOMETOWN:	Spring Lake Heights, NJ
BIKE(S) CURRENTLY USED:	Haro
MAJOR ACCOMPLISHMENTS IN FREESTYLE:	Still having fun riding! Freestyle helped set me up for all my major accomplishments in life!
PAST SPONSORS:	None, unless you include the local bike shops where we used to beg for free gyro cables, tubes & stickers!
FAVORITE RIDING AREA:	Any flat, somewhat dry spot with good vibes!
NON-BMX HEROES:	God, my wife Jean, Family, Friends, Yoda.
HOBBIES: (OTHER THAN RIDING)	Anything outdoors with Jean and our friends, 80s arcade games and pinball, surfing, snowboarding, sailing, <u>flying</u>.

PILOT
instagram.com/mattdaviator

MOON BABES OF BICYCLE CITY

Appendix

FULL MOONS
(2019 – 2043)

Sunday, October 13, 2019
Saturday, October 31, 2020
Wednesday, October 20, 2021
Sunday, October 9, 2022
Saturday, October 28, 2023
Thursday, October 17, 2024
Monday, October 6, 2025
Sunday, October 25, 2026
Friday, October 15, 2027
Tuesday, October 3, 2028
Monday, October 22, 2029
Friday, October 11, 2030
Thursday, October 30, 2031
Monday, October 18, 2032
Saturday, October 8, 2033
Friday, October 27, 2034
Tuesday, October 16, 2035
Sunday, October 5, 2036
Friday, October 23, 2037
Tuesday, October 12, 2038
Monday, October 31, 2039
Friday, October 19, 2040
Wednesday, October 9, 2041
Tuesday, October 28, 2042
Sunday, October 18, 2043

"MBOctober!!!" —The Pilot

RANDOM DISRUPTIVE SEQUENCE OF EVENTS

4/3/2019 BOOK BUNDLE PREORDER GOES LIVE
on mikedaily.bandcamp.com

Kit includes two 12"x18" poster prints of 2-Hip Cordoba card stock model car (concept by Mike Daily, art by Patrick Richardson), Bike Club t-shirt, post cards, Miami Hopper Yoga flyers, stickers in stacks, page from writing notebook, and typewritten thank you note + *Moon Babes of Bicycle City* (10/11/2019) upon publication as a 4"x7" paperback with names of BC members printed in the novel

Audio tracks of Chapter 1 feat. Bobby Loveless and Chapter 2 with Col. Patson release on mikedaily.bandcamp.com

4/13/2019 MAURICE MEYER POSTS PHOTOS
"Fun with paper craft Cordoba for Mike Daily's Moon Babes of Bicycle City book."

Dennis Dowling

4/17/2019 BOOK BUNDLE PREORDER CLOSES
with 43 Bike Club Members

5/1/2019 KITS SHIP

RANDOM DISRUPTIVE SEQUENCE OF EVENTS

7/15/2019 JAMES WHITE POSTS VIDEO

"A little visual interpretation of @moon.babes.of.bicycle.city"

7/19/2019 FRANK GARRIDO'S BIRTHDAY

7/31/2019 THE PLYWOOD HOODS PRESENT
Stoke&Word Pop Up Jam! in York, PA

Daily recites Chapters 1 and 2 with DJ Eaton

Jason Michael

8/8/2019 AUDIO TRACK OF CHAPTER X FEAT. STEVE BARONE RELEASES on mikedaily.bandcamp.com

9/27/2019 FIRST PRINTING, 100 Copies

Book Bundle Preorder 2.0 is offered online and direct by phone

Book Bundle 2.0 includes Bikecar Club t-shirt and vinyl stickers + signed copy of MBoBC

9/28/2019 THE HOMIE LUNGMUSTARD POSTS
David Blaine-style video

RANDOM DISRUPTIVE SEQUENCE OF EVENTS

10/2/2019   **AUDIO TRACK OF CHAPTER 9 FEAT. PROGENY RELEASES** on mikedaily.bandcamp.com

10/4/2019   **BOOK BUNDLE 2.0 (AND BOOKS FOR 1.0) SHIP** with surprise extras: 8.5"x11" BikeCardoba Prints (concept by Daily, art by Nathan Powell Design), paper dolls of Dizz Hicks and Ceppie Maes with standers, vinyl stickers, vintage comic books, and Double Bubble

10/9/2019   **ERIK MATSUNAGA POSTS** time-elapsed video of himself building the '76 Chrysler Cordoba

10/10/2019   **LYRIC VIDEO (CHAPTERS 9 AND 10) EPISODE AIRS** on Radio Concuss in Seattle

Friday, 10/11/2019   **STREET DATE OF MOON BABES OF BICYCLE CITY**

Daily receives letter and Roots Art from Craig Grasso

Grasso becomes MBoBCBC Member #099

> 10-8-19
> MIKE DAILY WOW BRO,
> IT'S BEEN OVER 20 YEARS SINCE I LAST HEARD FROM ANY OF THE INFAMOUS PLYWOOD HOODS. WHAT'S GOOD IN THE HOOD HOMEBOY. I HOPE ALL IS WELL WITH YOU.

10/12/2019   **"WILKERSON'S HERE,"** Daily posts to Facebook

MIKE SARRIS POSTS PHOTOS

"Lawnmower earlier"

RANDOM DISRUPTIVE SEQUENCE OF EVENTS

10/14/2019 "HOFFMAN'S HERE,"
Daily posts to Facebook

"All the way from Oklahoma City, Oklahoma"

MATT BASS POSTS PHOTO with comment:

"I landed in OKC today for a shoot- I told the crew the only thing in OKC is Mat Hoffman the legend! We go out to dinner and who's sitting right next to us! We talked moon babes and he told me about this!"

10/15/2019 DAILY POSTS TO FACEBOOK

"Cosmic that I got Grasso's letter and drawings on Friday, 10/11/19, the release date of Moon Babes of Bicycle City. The action in the novel occurs on that day in Bicycle City, New Mexico. When I saw who the letter was from, I gasped for air. Bill Bunting heard me. I was on the phone with Bill when I checked my mail. Bill is on the cover of the book, photo by his wife Jo. The last time I received mail from Grasso was for this interview we did that ran in the 9th issue of our Plywood Hoods zine, Aggro Rag Freestyle Mag! (October 1987).

That's why I say. Strange Days.

I don't want to get too weird (too late) but look at the page numbers on the opening spread of the interview: 10/11."

RANDOM DISRUPTIVE SEQUENCE OF EVENTS

10/15/2019 **TERRY TENETTE AND BRIAN TUNNEY**
(cont.) **POST PHOTOS** as comments

10/16/2019 **DIMITRI KEARES (RADIUS BIKE) POSTS**
Book Bundle-unboxing video

10/18/2019 **JAMES WHITE POSTS** "Alfred Hitchcock" video

"Any chance I get.... Thanks @moon.babes.of.bicycle.city for this extraordinary book!"

10/19/2019 **BUNDLES ARE SOLD OUT**
MBoBC thanks everybody who supported and participated

11/12/2019 **MOON BABES OF BICYCLE CITY MEETS THE TERRADOME**
Joe Cicman, MBoBC Bike Club Member #076 as in '76 Chrysler Cordoba, announces the Moon Babes of Bicycle City Video Contest open to everyone across the planet

Contest Details:
1) Film an edit in 1 day
2) Post to YouTube
3) Share on FB and tag Mike D.
Deadline for entries: 12/13/2019
https://youtu.be/CilUoPwnA5A

"This is a promotional video - Joe Cicman bought his copy on day 1 and has been removed from qualifications in a manner similar to how he was removed from the FlatlandFuel pro team"

Friday, 4/3/2020 **REMASTERED EDITION OF MOON BABES OF BICYCLE CITY IS RELEASED** by Stovepiper Books Media

"You seem to enjoy the pilot angle, so I got a photo reading MBoBC high over York, PA!"
Matt D'Angelo

Afterword

Although we've never met, I feel I've known Mike Daily for the majority of my life. The Plywood Hoods—our childhood heroes from York, PA—seemed a world away from us growing up in North Jersey, but they were brought to life by Mike with words and images and by Mark Eaton on film in a way that made them familiar and approachable, while still mythical and legendary.

Our heroes from the early days showed us how to make something big and inspiring from just ideas, activities, and a lifestyle we're passionate about. Those of us who enjoy these creative outlets and culture are very fortunate. I'm thankful every day for this. For BMX. For what it was then—the '80s, the '90s, when we would spend entire days and most of the night outside riding and enjoying the simplicity of it all. We would come home just to sleep, or to watch videos while we waited for bike parts, mail order, C.O.D. Our bedroom walls were covered in unevenly hung torn-out magazine and 'zine pages, each of their four corners taped.

It was then and continues to be a life full of great friendships, community, creativity, challenge, and adventure. All of us who rode together remain lifelong friends. Not all of us still ride, but we remain connected through BMX. It's hard to not be sentimental about it. That was our childhood, our life, and who we have become.

That explains why in the cubby in our little cape's second floor at the Jersey shore, I have a box of 'zines, a bigger box of magazines, and a Vans box full of stickers from the BMX and skateboarding era my friends and I had the pleasure of growing up in. Also, a cabinet full of VHS tapes—many of them homemade, some classics, some over-produced, but most lovingly budget-constrained and under-produced, from the era—slowly degrading as the tape erodes and transfers to itself.

When someone puts their heart and soul and spirit and experience and energy into such a creative and well-written book / time capsule / experience about an incredible era of BMX, that is something to support and share. That is why when Mike Daily launched his *Moon Babes of Bicycle City* (MBoBC) pre-order, I was up early before work on April, 3, 2019 (4/3), excited with anticipation, and I ordered two copies: one to read, enjoy, play with, and share, and another for the archive.

It was happenstance that I became MBoBC Bike Club Member Number 001. I was lucky to have ordered at the exact moment that Mike launched his capsule into the universe on that very early Wednesday morning in Oregon, slightly less early in New Mexico, and just before sunrise in Southern New Jersey, at the shore where in less than a week, my wife and I would learn that not only were we pregnant, but pregnant with triplets, who would be born less than a week after the books arrived at our home. The books arrived just before the Full Moon of Sunday, October 13th. The babies arrived just after. MBOctober. Moon Babes. Many Babies.

Jean and I were going to name our children after hub and rim makers in Japan, but when Rodd and Chat stole our thunder and named their daughters Suzue, Araya, and Ukai, we went with Italian family names, instead...Lucy, Sam, and Mary!

I was elated to be MBoBC Bike Club Number 001 and would have been just as happy to be Member Number 043, or simply to let Mike know how much we all appreciate what he does, who he is, and how much he has contributed to BMX and enriched our lives through his art and ingenuity.

The MBoBCBC Kit is a rad collection of STACKS of original and repop stickers, Bicycle City, NM post cards, original ads for Miami Hopper Yoga, and signed build-it-yourself paper 1976 Chrysler Cordobas from Ron Wilkerson's "moment in time in the world," 2-Hip Meet the Street, Santee, California, April 30, 1988. SoCal.

Moon Babes is a fun read full of bike lore, road trips, and BMX history. The style is Spike Jonze meets Tony Hillerman,[4] or, as Mike Daily puts it, "*RAD* meets *Breaking Bad*." Its enthusiasm, detail, and storytelling style remind me of *Beastie Boys Book* (2019), which isn't just a book about the Beastie Boys, just as MBoBC isn't just a book about BMX or the era of BMX many of us grew up in. It's a book about exploration, creativity, and connections. It builds context beautifully. More importantly, its pages seek and succeed in taking the written word and creating shared experiences. SoCial.

---

[4] Anthony Grove "Tony" Hillerman (May 27, 1925 – October 26, 2008) was an American author of detective novels and non-fiction works best known for his Navajo Tribal Police mystery novels. Several of his works have been adapted as theatrical and television movies.

To showcase Mike Daily's love of detail and endless creativity, Chapter X of the *Moon Babes* audiobook even ends with the beautiful dull thuddy click of a cassette recorder clicking off at the end of a dubbed mix tape or tape-to-tape edit...appropriate with how rhythmic and poetic the audiobook production is. Rakimestry.

Our babies haven't yet said their first words. I think each of them has said "DaDa" and "Daddy" already but that's under investigation by Mommy. Mary allegedly said, "Let's play!" when she was just a month old. Appropriate. Feels like just yesterday they were in the NICU in NYC and fit in the palms of our hands. At three months, they turned up the smiles for Mommy and Daddy. Big time. That makes us smile even more. Such little blessings and truly a miracle that everyone is healthy. Soon they'll be crawling, walking, talking, reading, writing, riding...

More than ever, we're realizing time goes by very quickly. We do our best to enjoy, treasure, and live each moment and appreciate the people we share those moments with. Mike Daily is one of the most present, caring, observant, and imaginative people we know. He has inspired my friends and me for decades with his gifts of creativity and storytelling. We hope our kids each find that thing, like BMX and skateboarding, that fulfills them and leads to lifelong friendships, connections, and the drive to constantly be creative.

THANK YOU, Mike! Stay rad! 🙏🖤🚲

Matt D'Angelo
Spring Lake Heights, New Jersey
February 7, 2020

,O'GRAPHY

🌀 O'GRAPHY

#1
BMX RAG
(1984)
Red Lion, PA
6" x 8"

#2
AGGRO RAG!
(1984)
Red Lion, PA
8" x 10 ½"

#3
AGGRO RAG!
(January 1985)
Red Lion, PA
8" x 10 ½"

#4
AGGRO RAG
FREESTYLE MAG!
(March 1985)
Red Lion, PA
5 ½" x 8 ½"

#5
*AGGRO RAG
FREESTYLE MAG!*
(Summer 1986)
York, PA
5 ½" x 8 ½"

#6
*AGGRO RAG
FREESTYLE MAG!*
(Fall 1986)
York, PA
5 ½" x 8 ½"

#7
*AGGRO RAG
FREESTYLE MAG!*
(January 1987)
York, PA / Lock Haven, PA
5 ½" x 8 ½"

#8
*AGGRO RAG
FREESTYLE MAG!*
(March 1987)
York, PA / Lock Haven, PA
5 ½" x 8 ½"

O'GRAPHY

#9
***AGGRO RAG
FREESTYLE MAG!***
(October 1987)
York, PA / Lock Haven, PA
5 ½" x 8 ½"

#10
***AGGRO RAG
FREESTYLE MAG!***
(Spring 1988)
York, PA / Lock Haven, PA
5 ½" x 8 ½"

#11
***AGGRO RAG
FREESTYLE MAG!***
(Summer 1988)
York, PA / Stamford, CT
5 ½" x 8 ½"

#12
***AGGRO RAG
FREESTYLE MAG!***
(Summer 1989)
York, PA
5 ½" x 8 ½"

STOVEPiPER: Book One (1994)

Anthology edited and published by Mike Daily.
Poetry. Prose. 144 pages.

Center Section (33 Poems): "The Poets Are All Lairs" by Steve Richmond.

Contributors: Greg Barbera, David Barker, Charles Bukowski, Neeli Cherkovski, Ana Christy, Jim Dewitt, Keith Dodson, Douglas Goodwin, Marvin Malone, Bill Shields, Hugh Brown Shu, Irving Stettner, Merle Tofér, Mark Weber, Jeff Weddle.

"Got your second letter...I sent you some shit (?) a couple of days ago. Never trust a writer's past record. Most fall apart quite quickly. Luck with Stovepiper."

—**Charles Bukowski** in a letter to Mike Daily ('93)

Valley (1998)

Mike Daily's first novel designed and published by Andy Jenkins/Bend Press.

Drifting through his days in a haze while attempting to make sense of mysteries unraveling before him—from the oddball people he meets in Affordable Student Housing (ASH) to the margin scribblings, receipts, and photos he happens upon in used books by his favorite authors—BMX magazine editor and college student Mick O'Grady reflects on life, love, and literature in the San Fernando Valley.

Softcover (Matte finish), 208 pages, First Edition, New Unread Condition. Signed copy with vintage enclosures. Also signed by Andy Jenkins.

"Mike Daily packs so many stylistic smash cuts into *Valley*, MTV dulls by comparison."—***RAY GUN MAGAZINE***

"[*Valley* is] an epic of fragmentation and disjointed thought processes, cutting in fits from genre to genre (screenplay, poetry, journalism, even college science lecture), with deliberately unrelenting commentary in the form of writing in the margins, footnotes, snapshots, bludgeoning headline-size type, and illustrations bleeding off the page. It should logically be a jarring, disjointed read. Miraculously it isn't. The reason is Daily's uncanny fluidity and rhythm."—**Brian Baltin**, *Blend Magazine*

"American readers might not readily recognize the reference but *Valley* immediately brought to mind Nick Hornby's *High Fidelity*. While Hornby is a music obsessive Daily is books crazy. He knows his Beat and literary history and his mind is a fascinating archive." —**Kevin Ring**, *Beat Scene Magazine*

ꓝ O'GRAPHY

the VALLEY AUDIO PROJECT
Released May 15, 1999

Excerpts from Mike Daily's novel *Valley* (1998, Bend Press) as read by the author with Jennifer Affronti.

Cover Design by Andy Jenkins. Presented by Bend Press in association with Lunchbox in Torrance, CA.

Voice of "Newscaster" is Dan McKee.
Voice of "Freya" is Jennifer Affronti.
Voice of "Mick" is Mike Daily.

Mixed live by Simon James, San Fernando Valley, CA, May 1999.

ALL THE RIGHT MOVES, ALL THE WRONG NOTES: THE LIFTER PULLER STORY (2000)

Mike Daily's LFTR PLLR rock journalism published by Stovepiper Books.

Zine. 3.75" x 4.25", 48 pages, stapled.

Complete & Unexpurgated.

"Korean Grass Never Needs to Be Cut" / "Drum Machines"
(Mike Daily & Roads Less Traveled)
Released May 5, 2005

Mike Daily recorded two songs with Portland rock/funk band Roads Less Traveled. Daily recited his poem "Korean Grass Never Needs to Be Cut" on RLT's song "Section 8" and RLT improvised a jam for Daily's recitation of "Drum Machines."

Cover: Nathan Powell Design

Mastered by Antreo Pukay at Tell Tale Recording in Portland, Oregon.

MAJOR FICTION

(Daily, Moscovich & Strahota / O'GRADY)
Released June 20, 2006

"Mike Daily and Co. have produced Major Fiction. It's a great (and long) track that mentions every title put out by FC2 (and its predecessor, Fiction Collective). Since it's endorsed by FC2, and even Raymond Federman, you simply must check it out."—*Fade Theory*

Cover Design by Matthew Revert.

DAILY, MOSCOVICH & STRAHOTA
Mike Daily (lyrics-collage of all Fiction Collective, FC2 & Black Ice book titles up to October 5, 2005, vocals)
David Noel Moscovich (keyboard, hand-held digital recorder, samples, distortion, toy steering wheel)
Luke Strahota (banter at the beginning, Boss DR 660 drum machine, drum kit)
Mia (the diva)

Recorded by Chutz Ponderosa at The Enginehouse
in Portland, Oregon, on October 5, 2005.

Mastered by Antreo Pukay at Tell Tale Recording in Portland, Oregon.

Kevin Sampselliana: Pt. I / Pt. II

(O'GRADY Ft. Kevin Sampsell)
Released June 7, 2007

"Kevin Sampselliana" is a two-part indie rock selection from Mike Daily's novel and double CD set, *ALARM* (2007) recorded in Portland, Oregon, by the author with his band, O'GRADY.

Cover: Nathan Powell Design

Stephen Kurowski took the author's photo of Kevin Sampsell printed on the back cover of *How to Lose Your Mind with the Lights On* (1994).

O'GRADY FT. KEVIN SAMPSELL
Mike Daily: Fiction
Adam Levi Hungate: Guitar God
Chutz Ponderosa: Bass
Kevin Sampsell: Kevin Sampsell
Luke Strahota: Drums

"Kevin Sampselliana" was recorded at The Enginehouse
in Portland, Oregon, in 2006.

Mastered by Antreo Pukay, Tell Tale Recording.

BI O'GRAPHY

ALARM (2007)

Mike Daily's second novel published by Stovepiper Books Media.

Book includes two full-length CDs (one studio album, one compilation of live performances). Thirty-six tracks. Daily tipped in newspaper clippings over the disc-holder pockets inside the front and back covers.

Riveted Edition (spine reinforced with aluminum rivets).

Terror Musical Collage Sticker: Kevin Sampsell.

"*ALARM* is a fantastically real account of life as we know it—and especially succeeds at uncovering the humor and magic of our most normal days working, loving, and living." —**Craig Finn, The Hold Steady**

"Authentic as Harvey Pekar's graphic novels, as energetic and raw as any new indie movement, *ALARM* is a novel in the form of a rock song or a rock song in the form of a novel that mines the humor in mainstream culture as well as the humor in underground culture—along with their anthrax concerns, adverting pitches, boy-girl problems, and all the rest of the mashup."—**Steve Tomasula**, author of *VAS: An Opera in Flatland*

"What started with Patchen and Rexroth when they combined reading with jazz music, and what continued on through Kerouac and Ginsberg, through Jim Morrison and Patti Smith, through Jello Biafra, Henry Rollins, and Genesis P-Orridge, continues with renewed vigor and a fresh voice through the work of Mike Daily and his band, O'GRADY."—**Eckhard Gerdes**, author of *My Landlady the Lobotomist*

ALARM Album

(Mike Daily / O'GRADY)
Released July 7, 2007

A man and a woman in Southern California's San Fernando Valley wrangle with relationship concerns in the immediate aftermath of the 9/11 terrorist attacks. Listen to selections from Mike Daily's novel and double CD set, *ALARM* (2007) recorded in Portland, Oregon, by the author with his band, O'GRADY.

Cover: Nathan Powell Design
Photo: Ryan Schierling
Terror Musical Collage Sticker: Kevin Sampsell.

O'GRAPHY

ALARM: NOVEL AS PERFORMANCE (2006-2007)

Released July 8, 2007

Racing, braking, being stuck in traffic, laughing. Impatient. Los Angeles. L.A. Selections from Mike Daily's novel, *ALARM* (2007) recited live in Portland, Oregon, by the author with his band, O'GRADY.

Cover: Nathan Powell Design
Photo: Linda Kay Lund

"Just when it seems as if America's literary heart has flatlined, Mike Daily steals in with paddles and electroshock. Creating a category all his own between sound and text, Daily hums along like an electrical current zapping every territory of the social body—consumer culture, media wasteland, relationship see-saws, and oh yeah, the so-called 'self.'" —**Lidia Yuknavitch,** author of *The Book of Joan*

"Projective, post-jazz, post-rock prose." —**Yuriy Tarnawsky,** author of *Three Blondes & Death*

"Your stuff deals with people. You're one of them, but only to the extent you relate to others and the world. I love the energy. I love the synthesis, the production, the action." —**Jerome Klinkowitz,** author of *Vonnegut in Fact: The Public Spokesmanship of Personal Fiction*

"MR VICED HONEST / STEVE RICHMOND"
Live Recitation

Released May 28, 2009

Mike Daily recited "MR VICED HONEST / STEVE RICHMOND" for Portland Aggressive: An Evening of Tough Love at Ella Street Social Club in Portland, Oregon, on May 28, 2009. "MR VICED HONEST" is an anagram of "STEVE RICHMOND."

Cover: Nathan Powell Design

Photo of Steve Richmond and Mike Daily at Richmond's house in Santa Monica, CA, by Kelly O'Donnell, 1994.

DO'GRAPHY

"MR VICED HONEST / STEVE RICHMOND" EP

Released September 9, 2009

Mike Daily wrote "MR VICED HONEST / STEVE RICHMOND" about Steve Richmond and Richmond's gagaku music-influenced poems. Daily recorded this grungy six-song EP in Portland, Oregon, with his band, MR VICED HONEST. "Hidden Track" alert.

Cover: Nathan Powell Design
MR VICED HONEST
Guitar: Adam Levi Hungate
Bass: Chutz Ponderosa
Electronics: Foots
Drums: Luke Strahota
Lyrics/Vocals: Mike Daily

Mastered by Antreo Pukay, Tell Tale Recording

"For those of you relatively recent to the small press scene, the name of Steve Richmond may be unfamiliar. Steve was, in his day, one of the small press giants; a close friend of Bukowski, published by d.a. levy of Cleveland among many, many others, Steve was part of the original mimeograph small press revolution of the 60's which grew out of the Beats into one of the great counterculture movements in US history."
—**Don Wentworth**, *Lilliput Review*

Gagaku Meat: The Steve Richmond Story (2009)

Published by Stovepiper Books Media.

8-1/2 x 11, 32 Pages, Stapled.

"This little book reads like a crazy author biography/mystery. Thoroughly researched and endlessly fascinating, *Gagaku Meat* covers the wild history of poet Steve Richmond, with ties to Bukowski, Jim Morrison, and the underground small press scene of the 60s, 70s, and 80s. Daily has reconnected with many of Richmond's colleagues, who offer insight to Richmond's up-and-down writing career. This book is also beautifully designed with a lot of photos, letter fragments, and the like. I'm not a big Richmond fan myself, but this is still an interesting and tragic read that fans of renegade writers will enjoy."
—**Kevin Sampsell**, Future Tense Books

"The essential prose on Steve Richmond."—**Todd Moore**

"Now You Can Sleep" feat. Jase Daniels & Gasoline Monk

Released October 10, 2010

Cover Design by Matthew Revert.

Gasoline Monk made the beat.

Mike Daily wrote and spoke the words.

Jase Daniels produced "Now You Can Sleep."

Mastered by Antreo Pukay at Tell Tale Recording in Portland, Oregon.

NOW YOU CAN SLEEP

It was our last night together. I couldn't sleep. I drank too much coffee, ate too much shredded wheat. You should have had decaf. It's not the same. It's late. It's not that late. Come here. Now you can sleep.

I couldn't sleep. I didn't fight it. I didn't have to be awake the next day for anything. We had to check out by 11am. I knew where some food was. I had some sweet Hawaiian dinner rolls and a banana in a bag.

I filled a cup with water.

I couldn't find the CD I got at the mall.

Now you can sleep.

I asked her if she wanted me to turn on the TV so she didn't have to hear me fidgeting around.

Nah, she said. It's ok.

I picked up the remote and pressed power anyway. I knew that TV helped her sleep. I was going to be awake for some time.

I couldn't find the CD I got at the mall.

Now you can sleep.

I found the CD. It was buried in my backpack. Under some shirts.

"Beckett" feat. Jase Daniels & Gasoline Monk

Released April 13, 2011

Cover Design by Jase Daniels.

Gasoline Monk made the beat.

Mike Daily wrote and spoke the words.

Jase Daniels produced "Beckett."

Mastered by Antreo Pukay at Tell Tale Recording in Portland, Oregon.

BECKETT

One look and the fear is on. The fear. Beckett. The man elicits fear. Even the look of him. But moreso the books of him. Words. Works. Even the name. Samuel Beckett. Who thinks of the plays? It's the books. One look and the fear is on. The fear. Beckett. It's fearsome. Ominous. *More Pricks Than Kicks. Murphy. Molloy. Malone Dies.* Now I'm on *The Unnamable.* Federman said to read *How It Is* next. It's "fidge"--that's why I like it. I'm sure it's more fidge in the French. Word plays and so forth. The fidge in English is mighty. Mighty fine. Funny. Beckett. He translated *Molloy, Malone Dies,* and *The Unnamable* from the French.

He wrote the shite in French. Irishman Beckett. Imagine the brogue. Rogue. He's a rogue. Beckett. Samuel Beckett. The look of him is stark. Spiked. Birdlike. I was beginning to understand Federman's fascination with Sam. *Murphy* is explosively funny for the reader. What restraint and lyrical intelligence Beckett displays. I read that he reached a point where he stopped trying to not be depressed and oppose that part of himself. After all, it was he who said there is nothing funnier than unhappiness. Beckett. One look and the fear is on. The fear. Beckett.

'O'GRAPHY

#13
AGGRO RAG FREESTYLE MAG!
The Hip-Hop Issue Number 13
(October 2012)
Beaverton, OR
5 ½" x 8 ½"

For the first issue of *Aggro Rag* zine to appear since '89, Mike Daily interviewed 15 of the most innovative flatlanders from the fluorescent era of freestyle. Each copy of this limited edition of 500 was signed by Plywood Hoods Brett Downs, Mark Eaton, Kevin Jones, Jamie McKulik, Dale Mitzel, and *AR* Editor Daily. Covers were individually autographed in gold paint pen ink by InTRIKat, Chad Johnston.

Pictured left: Jeff Tremaine with *Aggro Rag* Issue 13

Mike Daily Interview by Anthony Buglio for FlatWebTV
(Podcast Edition)
Released March 6, 2013

"Mike Daily, original Plywood Hood member and creator of *Aggro Rag Freestyle Mag!* sat down with FlatWebTV to talk about the release of his book (the collection of issues 1-12 of *Aggro Rag*), his history producing the 'zine and the collaboration with Subrosa to release an *Aggro Rag* edition of the 2013 Subrosa DTT. *Aggro Rag* is an amazing piece of history and this interview brings some of those stories to life."—**FlatWebTV**

Cover: Nathan Powell Design

Presented by FlatWebTV in Collaboration with Community in Portland, Oregon.

Camera and Edit by Anthony Buglio and Mark Rainha.

Featured Guest via Skype: Mark Eaton

Music in Intro and during Interview by Gasoline Monk: "Tripping My Head Off" and "Spring Fever."

Music in Outro/Credits by O'GRADY: "Kevin Sampselliana Pt. II" taken from the CD accompanying the novel, *ALARM*, by Mike Daily.

Mastered by Antreo Pukay at Tell Tale Recording in Portland, Oregon.

O'GRAPHY

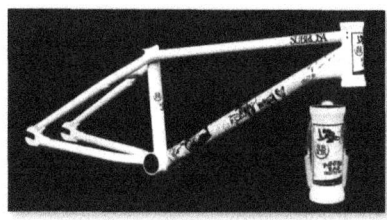

SUBROSA X AGGRO RAG DTT (DOUBLE TOP TUBE) FLATT & STREETT FRAMES (2013)

Limited Edition of 43
(21 FlatTT, 22 StreeTT)

Material: 4130 Sanko chromoly, double butted down tube, straight gauge top tubes, seat stays, chain stays

Top Tube: 19" for FlaTT; 21" for StreeTT

Chain Stay: 13.25" with room to remove wheel, 13" fully slammed for FlaTT; 13.75" and 13.5" respectively for StreeTT

Head Tube: 75 degrees, integrated, CNC Machined, heat treated, drilled for gyro tabs

Seat Tube: 71 degrees, internally and externally butted, 8.5" height, integrated seat clamp w/replaceable nut and bolt

BB Type: Mid, T5 Deathproof heat treated, specifically designed to not hang up during grinds

BB Height: 11.6", low profile removable brake mounts

Dropouts: 6mm investment cast hollow dropout w/integrated chain adjustor for 14mm axle, T5 Deathproof heat treated

Weight: 4.7 lbs for FlaTT; 5.1 lbs for StreeTT

Colors: White

Decals: Designed from *Aggro Rag Freestyle Mag!* zine graphics by Chip Riggs with Mike Daily

Aggro Rag Freestyle Mag! Plywood Hoods Zines '84-'89: The Complete Collection (2013) by Mike Daily

Published by Stovepiper Books Media.

Aggro Rag Freestyle Mag! Plywood Hoods Zines '84-'89: The Complete Collection contains all 12 issues of the underground BMX freestyle fanzine that rider and indie publisher Mike Daily made from '84 through '89. Limited to small print runs from the Xerox machine at a local video games arcade in York, PA, *Aggro Rag* was distributed at shows, AFA/2-Hip contests or by mail. Now is your chance to get them all in one comprehensive volume featuring exclusive new interviews with Kevin Jones and Dave Mirra; previously unpublished photos of Plywood Hoods and friends; classic interviews with innovative flatland and street riders including Gary Pollak, Craig Grasso, Ceppie Maes, Dizz Hicks, Jason Parkes and Pete Augustin; plenty of "fidge" and more. 43 footnotes! Foreword by Andy Jenkins. Introduction by Mark Lewman.

443 pages.

"If you own a copy of the A-Rag, you've got probably THE premier freestyle 'zine."
—*FREESTYLIN' Magazine,* April '88

∫ O'GRAPHY

The following are excerpts from the paperback *Moon Babes of Bicycle City,* available now from Stovepiper Books Media. "*RAD* meets *Breaking Bad* in Bicycle City, New Mexico."

Moon Babes of Bicycle City, Novel, Chapter 1
featuring **Bobby Loveless**

Cover Design: Patrick Richardson

Beat, Music, Backing Vocals: Bobby Loveless

Mastered by: Antreo Pukay at Tell Tale Recording

Novel: Mike Daily

Moon Babes of Bicycle City, Novel, Chapter 2
with **Col. Patson**

Cover Design: Matthew Revert

Illustration: Fetus

Music: Col. Patson

Intro: Shut-Ins

Mastered by: Antreo Pukay at Tell Tale Recording

Fiction: Mike Daily

4/3/19

U.K. Review by **James White**

My school teachers always remarked how awful my English was and that I should read more books. Well... I didn't! I read BMX magazines. Fast forward to today and I still haven't read a single piece of fictional literature.

So imagine my horror when one of the most important BMX journalists of my time asks me to review a couple of audio excerpts of his new book. Do I come clean and tell him I'm a book virgin, who blags his way through adolescence life, desperately hiding his Ignorance.

No I'll keep schtum. I've made it this far without being found out. "I've got this" I say to my self as I press play.

Damn right I've got this. Nowhere. And I mean nowhere! Will you ever hear anything like this. A story, using BMX word play, strung together in a completely surreal yet weirdly familiar way.

O'GRAPHY

At times poetic, at others it's just flat out freaky. This had me smiling one second then in awe of word play the next, all the while being completely immersed in this strange tale.

Based around the most anarchic and experimental contest to ever happen in BMX history, this, is exactly that, an exploration of BMXism's from a time period when BMX stood for 'make your own rules'. If there was ever a book to take my reading virginity then it's this one. Bang it home Mike!

Moon Babes of Bicycle City Bike Club Kit is going to be offered as a limited edition, which comes with a card model of that ever important car. So cool. Preorder today, check it out at MD's band camp.

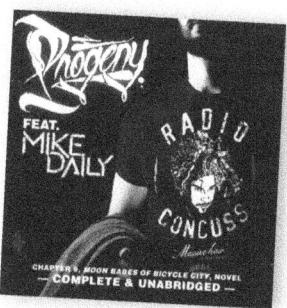

Moon Babes of Bicycle City, Novel, Chapter 9 by Progeny feat. Mike Daily

Cover: Nathan Powell Design

Beats, Music, & Live Mixing: Progeny

Mastered by: Antreo Pukay at Tell Tale Recording

Fiction: Mike Daily

Moon Babes of Bicycle City, Novel, Chapter X feat. Steve Barone

Cover: Nathan Powell Design

Jacket Zipper Scratching, Backing Vocals & Sound Design: Steve Barone

Drums: Misha Dashevsky

Guitar: Al Weiers

Steve Barone Band recorded with Chad Wheeling at Triple T Studio in Brooklyn Center, Minnesota

Produced & Mastered by: Antreo Pukay at Tell Tale Recording

Fiction: Mike Daily

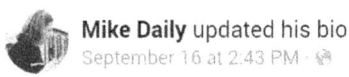

Mike Daily updated his bio.
September 16 at 2:43 PM

Air

Alice in Chains, Hollywood Palladium, Los Angeles, California, December 15, 1992

Mike Daily

Mark Eaton, 7/31/2019

Mike Daily is an author, journalist, zinemaker, and co-founder of the Plywood Hoods Freestyle BMX Trick Team. *Moon Babes of Bicycle City* (2020) is his third novel.

```
    keep it going, kid. it could be anytime. I mean, the end or the
beginning.
```

Buk

Charles Bukowski
in a letter to **Steve Richmond**
May 6, 1966

Now let's get a little marginal.

Craig Finn
"Candy's Room," *Fiestas + Fiascos* (1999),
Lifter Puller

www.ingramcontent.com/pod-product-compliance
Lightning Source LLC
Chambersburg PA
CBHW050031090426
42735CB00022B/3453